"Come up Hither"….
REVELATION 4:1

TIMOTHY E. MILLER

authorHOUSE®

AuthorHouse™
1663 Liberty Drive
Bloomington, IN 47403
www.authorhouse.com
Phone: 833-262-8899

Published by AuthorHouse 05/18/2021

ISBN: 978-1-7283-2136-3 (sc)
ISBN: 978-1-7283-2135-6 (e)

Scripture taken from The Holy Bible, King James Version.

An e book about the Rapture titled:

"Come up hither"…...Rev 4:1

Answers four Questions:

1. What is the Rapture?
2. Why is there a Rapture?
3. When will it occur?
4. What time is it now?

CONTENTS

PREFACE

This short e book is not an exhaustive study of the Rapture but is limited to answering the following four questions about the Rapture:

- What is the Rapture?
- Why is there a Rapture?
- When will it occur?
- What time is it now?

The reason for this writing is to rebut some internet blogs recently written regarding the end of the age. The blogs are mentioned in greater detail in the Introduction and you are encouraged to review them on your own. On the eve of the failed prediction of the blogs there were about one million readers and from some of their comments one can see how convinced they were that the end was imminent. I wrote a few emails to the blogger telling her that the information that she was providing was false but my comments fell on deaf ears. Some of the information I provided is contained in the introduction.

In addition to rebuttal of the bloggers it is also my hope that readers will get a better understanding of the Rapture and take their own initiative to read what the Bible says about that point in time when Jesus retrieves his Church from the earth. This is the only way to keep from being deceived in these end of days.

All of the Bible verses cited in the answers to the questions are from the King James Version.

INTRODUCTION

For several months in 2013 I was following internet posts from Bon on Bon's Blog, Hearing From God; and posts from Julie on Behold I Come. Together they had more than a million viewers. At the time of this writing the posts are still available on their web sites. Bon was writing from Australia and Julie was writing from the United States. They both claim to be hearing from God independently and both have essentially identical messages. My summary of their messages is as follows:

1. In the very near future there will be a cosmic disturbance in the sky that the whole world will see. They have not said so, but I believe that they were counting on Comet Ison to cause that event. Because of her last message from God, Bon shut down her blog as of Nov 7, 2013, and warned people that the disturbance is coming soon. On November 28 the comet disintegrated due to the heat of the sun leaving no cosmic disturbance. There have been no further messages on Bon's blog. Julie has moved her family to an unknown location but continues

her blog. Both of the blogs are available for review on the internet. I encourage you to view them.

2. Following the disturbance in the sky there will be an earthquake of epic proportions.

3. Following the earthquake there will be no light on the earth for three days. Bon and Julie have given their followers specific instruction for that three-day period. During the three days of darkness God will speak to each individual in their spirit and each person will be given the opportunity to accept or reject Him.

4. Following the three days of darkness, those who are or have become believers will, for a brief period of time, evangelize the non-believers. Then the end will come.

So, in effect, this is God's final warning to man before He comes to remove his true Church. To some of you who are familiar with prophecy of Roman Catholic followers, it all sounds very similar to the Marian Apparitions of the twentieth century and earlier. The three days of darkness prophecy has also been around for centuries in Catholic circles.

I was alarmed when I read their blogs because I knew that their messages were inconsistent with the Olivet Discourse of Matthew 24. I contacted Bon by email to express my view but my information had no impact. Among other things, I told her that the Bible does call for a time when the Gospel will be preached in all the world (Mat 24:14) but that would not be until after the rapture. I further suggested that it was highly unlikely that the Gospel would be preached to the whole world both before and after the rapture. I believe that

Jesus laid out for us in the Olivet Discourse the events and the order in which they would happen prior to the end of the age and of His return. I also believe that Satan is alive and well and is deceiving as many people as he can. Deception is the main weapon that he will use to confuse Believers about the rapture. If these three events summarized above did not happen there would be a lot of people who would lose interest in watching for His return. This is not very different from the old story of the boy who cried wolf. That's why the Lord left us with His Word as a guide and why we should be like the Bereans in Acts 17 and search for truth and understanding so that we are not deceived.

In Acts 17:10-12 Paul was preaching to the Jews in the synagogue in Berea. The passage states that they eagerly received the word and examined the Scriptures to see if what Paul was preaching was true. Because of their personal examination of their scrolls many of them came to believe in Jesus as their Savior.

10 And the brethren immediately sent away Paul and Silas by night unto Berea: who coming thither went into the synagogue of the Jews.
11 These were more noble than those in Thessalonica, in that they received the word with all readiness of mind, and searched the scriptures daily, whether those things were so.
12 Therefore many of them believed; also of honourable women which were Greeks, and of men, not a few.

Much of the remaining information that I sent to her is contained in the body of the following book. It will not be repeated in the introduction.

I was very disturbed at the number of people who were eagerly following the posts of Bon and Julie. Their followers were blindly in agreement with the posts of Bon and Julie so I felt compelled to write the following in hope that people would not only read it but then go to the Bible and find out for themselves. Wanting people to read the scriptures for themselves is the reason that I have included them in the body of the book instead of just identifying the chapter and verse where they can be located.

QUESTION 1

What is the Rapture?

It is the gathering of God's own people to Himself. The following scripture verses describe the Rapture:

1 Thessalonians 4:13-18

¹³ But I would not have you to be ignorant, brethren, concerning them which are asleep, that ye sorrow not, even as others which have no hope.

¹⁴ For if we believe that Jesus died and rose again, even so them also which sleep in Jesus will God bring with him.

¹⁵ For this we say unto you by the word of the Lord, that we which are alive and remain unto the coming of the Lord shall not prevent them which are asleep.

¹⁶ For the Lord himself shall descend from heaven with a shout, with the voice of the archangel, and with the trump of God: and the dead in Christ shall rise first:

¹⁷ Then we which are alive and remain shall be caught up together with them in the clouds, to meet the Lord in the air: and so shall we ever be with the Lord.

¹⁸ Wherefore comfort one another with these words.

1 Corinthians 15:51-55

⁵¹Behold, I shew you a mystery; We shall not all sleep, but we shall all be changed,

⁵²In a moment, in the twinkling of an eye, at the last trump: for the trumpet shall sound, and the dead shall be raised incorruptible, and we shall be changed.

⁵³For this corruptible must put on incorruption, and this mortal must put on immortality.

⁵⁴So when this corruptible shall have put on incorruption, and this mortal shall have put on immortality, then shall be brought to pass the saying that is written, Death is swallowed up in victory.

⁵⁵O death, where is thy sting? O grave, where is thy victory?

The following portion of scripture describes the rapture of the church and events that occur in heaven immediately after the Rapture.

Revelation 4:1-6

4 After this I looked, and, behold, a door was opened in heaven: and the first voice which I heard was as it were of a trumpet talking with me; which said, Come up hither, and I will shew thee things which must be hereafter, (same as 1 Thes 4 and 1 Corinth 15)

² And immediately I was in the spirit: and, behold, a throne was set in heaven, and one sat on the throne.

³ And he that sat was to look upon like a jasper and a sardine stone: and there was a rainbow round about the throne, in sight like unto an emerald.

⁴ And round about the throne were four and twenty seats: and upon the seats I saw four and twenty elders sitting, clothed in white raiment; and they had on their heads crowns of gold. (attire of saints, Rev 19:8)

⁵ And out of the throne proceeded lightnings and thunderings and voices: and there were seven lamps of fire burning before the throne, which are the seven Spirits of God.

⁶ And before the throne there was a sea of glass like unto crystal: and in the midst of the throne, and round about the throne, were four beasts full of eyes before and behind.

Verse 1 explains the intent of the angel who accompanies John. This verse is very similar to the underlined verses in 1 Thes 4 and 1 Corin 15 above. John sees a door open and hears the sound of a talking trumpet which tells him what will happen very soon. He then says that he is having a vision of a throne set in heaven. There is one sitting on the throne with a rainbow around the throne. The rainbow identifies the one sitting on the throne as God. In Gen 9 the rainbow was identified as a sign given to Noah that God would not again destroy the earth with a flood. There are 24 seats around the throne with 24 elders sitting on the thrones. The word elder also means a pastor, leader, or teacher in the church. Their identity is further disclosed when John says that they were wearing white robes and crowns of gold on their heads. In Rev 7:9-17 white robes are given to tribulation saints who are killed during the great tribulation and are standing around the throne. The gold crowns are rewards given to believers in heaven. There are 5 crowns mentioned in the New Testament. One can easily conclude that the elders are raptured or resurrected saints. In verse 6 John says that he sees a sea of glass around the throne that looks like crystal. The sea of glass is the raptured saints and they are identified in Revelation 5: 8-11. The saints are in heaven prior to the wrath of God that will come upon the world. The wrath will be described when the seals to the book are removed in Rev 6 below. Let's look at verses 8-11 first.

Revelation 5:8-11

[8] And when he had taken the book, the four beasts and four and twenty elders fell down before the Lamb, having every one of them harps, and <u>golden vials full of odours, which are the prayers of saints.</u>

[9] And <u>they sung a new song</u>, saying, <u>Thou art worthy to take the book, and to open the seals thereof: for thou wast slain, and hast redeemed us to God by thy blood out of every kindred, and tongue, and people, and nation;</u> (Angels cannot sing this song, they are not redeemed and are not part of the church. It is a new song because the saints have just arrived in heaven from every kindred.......)

[10] And <u>hast made us unto our God kings and priests: and we shall reign on the earth.</u> (angels are not kings or priests, the saints are Rev1:6)

[11] And I beheld, <u>and I heard the voice of many angels round about the throne and the beasts and the elders: and the number of them was ten thousand times ten thousand, and thousands of thousands;</u> (same as Rev 6 & 7, Dan 7:10)

The first thing to notice here are the vials in verse 8 which are full of the prayers of the saints. Fast forward to Rev 8 and we see that these vials are full of the prayers of the saints and are used as part of the seventh seal judgement. The saints, even though referred to as angels, assist in the execution of these judgments. That is an interesting fact but may not be that useful in establishing that the sea of glass around the throne is the raptured and resurrected saints. However, it does help substantiate that the saints are in heaven during the tribulation for Israel. The use of the vials and the removal of the 7th seal are beyond the scope of this study and won't be mentioned again.

Now look at verse 9 and note that they are singing a new song. It is a new song not previously sung in heaven before because the saints have just arrived. It is a song of redemption. Angels have been in heaven but they cannot sing this new song because they have not been redeemed by the blood of God out of every kindred, and tongue, and people, and nation. Angels are not part of the church. In verse 11 John hears the voice of many angels singing the redemption song so if angels cannot sing this song then who is? The answer is that they have to be the raptured or resurrected saints. They are the sea of glass around the throne.

Now look at verse 10 which says that God has made us kings and priests and that we will rule with Him on the earth. Rev 1:6 confirms that the saints (born again believers) will be kings and priests; not the angels.

My hope is that thus far I have shown that the "sea of glass" around the throne is the resurrected and raptured saints and that the word "angels" is used to describe the saints.

I have a bit more evidence that the "sea of glass" is a reference to large groups of people and the "angels round about the throne" are really raptured and resurrected saints.

First the sea of glass.

Revelation 17:1 and 15

17 And there came one of the seven angels which had the seven vials, and talked with me, saying unto me, Come hither; I will shew unto thee the judgment of the great whore <u>that sitteth upon many waters</u>:

¹⁵ And he saith unto me, <u>The waters</u> which thou sawest, where the whore sitteth, <u>are peoples, and multitudes, and nations, and tongues.</u>

Verses 1 and 15 of Rev 17 tell us that there is a great whore that sitteth on many waters and the waters are defined as peoples, multitudes, nations, and tongues. Nothing more needs to be said.

Daniel 7:1-4, 17

In the first year of Belshazzar king of Babylon Daniel had a dream and visions of his head upon his bed: then he wrote the dream, and told the sum of the matters.

² Daniel spake and said, I saw in my vision by night, and, behold, <u>the four winds of the heaven strove upon the great sea.</u>

³ <u>And four great beasts came up from the sea, diverse one from another.</u>

¹⁷ <u>These great beasts, which are four, are four kings, which shall arise out of the earth.</u>

This portion of scripture describes world events at the time of the Rapture. Verses 2, 3, and 17 essentially say that there are 4 leaders which arise out of the sea (the earth). The obvious interpretation here is that the sea refers to the nations or peoples that the kings arise from.

Now for more evidence regarding the identity of the angles round about the throne. There are at least 3 other chapters of Revelation that use the word angel as other than an angelic being.

Revelation 1:18-20

I am he that liveth, and was dead; and, behold, I am alive for evermore, Amen; and have the keys of hell and of death.

¹⁹ Write the things which thou hast seen, and the things which are, and the things which shall be hereafter;

²⁰ <u>The mystery of the seven stars which thou sawest in my right hand, and the seven golden candlesticks. The seven stars are the angels of the seven churches: and the seven candlesticks which thou sawest are the seven churches</u>

Jesus is speaking to John in this passage. He is telling him to write the vision and in chapter 2 he is instructed to write a letter to each of the angels of the 7 churches. The angels of the 7 churches are not angelic beings. They are pastors or elders. Angels are not part of the church. For the most part, the churches are made up of born again believers for whom the letters were intended.

Revelation 10

10 *And I saw another mighty angel come down from heaven, clothed with a cloud: and a rainbow was upon his head, and his face was as it were the sun, and his feet as pillars of fire:* (see Rev 1:13-15)

2 And he had in his hand a little book open: and he set his right foot upon the sea, and his left foot on the earth, (with title deed in hand He takes possession)

3 And cried with a loud voice, as when a lion roareth: and when he had cried, seven thunders uttered their voices.

4 And when the seven thunders had uttered their voices, I was about to write: and I heard a voice from heaven saying unto me, Seal up those things which the seven thunders uttered, and write them not.

5 And the angel which I saw stand upon the sea and upon the earth lifted up his hand to heaven,

6 And sware by him that liveth for ever and ever, who created heaven, and the things that therein are, and the earth, and the things that therein are, and the sea, and the things which are therein, that there should be time no longer: (God owns what he has created and has declared that time is up. He has sent Jesus to reclaim the earth)

7 But in the days of the voice of the seventh angel, when he shall begin to sound, the mystery of God should be finished, as he hath declared to his servants the prophets.

8 And the voice which I heard from heaven spake unto me again, and said, Go and take the little book which is open in the hand of the angel which standeth upon the sea and upon the earth. (an act of possession)

⁹ And I went unto the angel, and said unto him, Give me the little book. And he said unto me, Take it, and eat it up, and it shall make thy belly bitter, but it shall be in thy mouth sweet as honey.

¹⁰ And I took the little book out of the angel's hand, and ate it up; and it was in my mouth sweet as honey: and as soon as I had eaten it, my belly was bitter.

¹¹ And he said unto me, Thou must prophesy again before many peoples, and nations, and tongues, and kings.

In this passage John sees a mighty angel come down from heaven. The first thing of interest in this vision is that John is now seeing things from the earth rather than from heaven. His description of the angel in verse 1 is similar to the description of Jesus in Rev 1. In addition, he has a rainbow on his head. Right away we can conclude that the angel is Jesus and not an angelic being. In Verse 2 he has a little book that is open in his hand. This has to be the same book which had the seven seals. From the context of this chapter we can conclude that the book is the title deed to the earth. Jesus was the only one qualified to remove the seals and now he has come to reclaim the earth. In Verse 5 and 6 the angel (Jesus) stands on the sea and the earth and takes possession. Lifting his hand to heaven, he swears by him who created the heavens and the earth that time shall be no longer. In effect, he is saying that God owns what he has created and he has declared that time is up. Jesus has been sent to reclaim the earth with the title deed in his hand. The angel in this case is Jesus.

Revelation 14

⁶And I saw another angel fly in the midst of heaven, having the everlasting gospel to preach unto them that dwell on the earth, and to every nation, and kindred, and tongue, and people,

⁷Saying with a loud voice, Fear God, and give glory to him; for the hour of his judgment is come: and worship him that made heaven, and earth, and the sea, and the fountains of waters. (Romans 10:17 faith comes by hearing of the word)

In Rev 14 the Gospel is being preached to every nation, kindred, tongue, and people. The time is after the Rapture and during the 42-month tribulation for people who become believers after the rapture. A parallel passage is from the Olivet Discourse in Matthew 24:14. This preaching of the Gospel to all the world is called the latter rain and will be discussed again in Chapter 3 of this book.

Matthew 24:14

¹⁴ And this gospel of the kingdom shall be preached in all the world for a witness unto all nations; and then shall the end come.

In verse 6 of Rev 14 above please note that the Gospel is being preached to the whole world by angels flying through the air. It is not being preached on the ground to the general population as it is now. What has changed is that born-again believers have been raptured and at the same time Satan has been cast to the earth. More about this event in Chapter 3 of this book. He is enraged at not being able to prevent the

Rapture. For 42 months Satan and his followers attempt to kill people who become believers after the Rapture. The people who are killed by Satan because of their testimony are identified as tribulation saints in Rev 7. It can be safely assumed that any preaching of the Gospel on the earth would be done in an underground manner.

Verse 6 identifies the preachers as angels but once again I assert that the word angel is being used by John as another word for raptured or resurrected Saints. The great commission to preach the Gospel was given to believers by Jesus in Matthew 28:18-20: *¹⁸ And Jesus came and spake unto them, saying, All power is given unto me in heaven and in earth. ¹⁹ Go ye therefore, and teach all nations, baptizing them in the name of the Father, and of the Son, and of the Holy Ghost: ²⁰ Teaching them to observe all things whatsoever I have commanded you: and, lo, I am with you always, even unto the end of the world. Amen.*

John 17:14-18 also indicates that Jesus was sent by God into the world and then Jesus sent us. *¹⁴ I have given them thy word; and the world hath hated them, because they are not of the world, even as I am not of the world. ¹⁵ I pray not that thou shouldest take them out of the world, but that thou shouldest keep them from the evil. ¹⁶ They are not of the world, even as I am not of the world. ¹⁷ Sanctify them through thy truth: thy word is truth. ¹⁸ As thou hast sent me into the world, even so have I also sent them into the world.*

We have always been the ones to spread the "Good News" and will continue until the end of the church age. Angels are not redeemed (born again) and are not part of the church.

In the book of Acts, chapters 8, 9 and 10, there are detailed accounts of the conversion of Paul, Cornelius, and the Ethiopian that show the involvement of both humans and angels in the conversion experience. In each case there were angels or spirits involved but it was disciples that taught or preached the Gospel. The reason for this is that God has committed His word of truth to be taught to the world by men and women who are born again into His family. That is why the angel flying in the midst of heaven preaching the everlasting Gospel in Rev 14:6 is not an angel at all but is a raptured or resurrected Saint.

Acts 8:26-39

26 And the angel of the Lord spake unto Philip, saying, Arise, and go toward the south unto the way that goeth down from Jerusalem unto Gaza, which is desert.

27 And he arose and went: and, behold, a man of Ethiopia, an eunuch of great authority under Candace queen of the Ethiopians, who had the charge of all her treasure, and had come to Jerusalem for to worship,

28 Was returning, and sitting in his chariot read Esaias the prophet.

29 Then the Spirit said unto Philip, Go near, and join thyself to this chariot.

30 And Philip ran thither to him, and heard him read the prophet Esaias, and said, Understandest thou what thou readest?

31 And he said, How can I, except some man should guide me? And he desired Philip that he would come up and sit with him.

³² The place of the scripture which he read was this, He was led as a sheep to the slaughter; and like a lamb dumb before his shearer, so opened he not his mouth.

³³ In his humiliation his judgment was taken away: and who shall declare his generation? for his life is taken from the earth.

³⁴ And the eunuch answered Philip, and said, I pray thee, of whom speaketh the prophet this? of himself, or of some other man?

³⁵ Then Philip opened his mouth, and began at the same scripture, and preached unto him Jesus.

³⁶ And as they went on their way, they came unto a certain water: and the eunuch said, See, here is water; what doth hinder me to be baptized?

³⁷ And Philip said, If thou believest with all thine heart, thou mayest. And he answered and said, I believe that Jesus Christ is the Son of God.

³⁸ And he commanded the chariot to stand still: and they went down both into the water, both Philip and the eunuch; and he baptized him.

³⁹ And when they were come up out of the water, the Spirit of the Lord caught away Philip, that the eunuch saw him no more: and he went on his way rejoicing.

Acts 9:10-20

¹⁰ And there was a certain disciple at Damascus, named Ananias; and to him said the Lord in a vision, Ananias. And he said, Behold, I am here, Lord.

¹¹ *<u>And the Lord said unto him, Arise, and go into the street which is called Straight, and enquire in the house of Judas for one called Saul, of Tarsus: for, behold, he prayeth,</u>*

¹² *<u>And hath seen in a vision a man named Ananias coming in, and putting his hand on him, that he might receive his sight</u>.*

¹³ *Then Ananias answered, Lord, I have heard by many of this man, how much evil he hath done to thy saints at Jerusalem:*

¹⁴ *And here he hath authority from the chief priests to bind all that call on thy name.*

¹⁵ *But the Lord said unto him, <u>Go thy way: for he is a chosen vessel unto me, to bear my name before the Gentiles, and kings, and the children of Israel:</u>*

¹⁶ *For I will shew him how great things he must suffer for my name's sake.*

¹⁷ *And Ananias went his way, and entered into the house; and putting his hands on him said, Brother Saul, the Lord, even Jesus, that appeared unto thee in the way as thou camest, hath sent me, that thou mightest receive thy sight, and be filled with the Holy Ghost.*

¹⁸ *And immediately there fell from his eyes as it had been scales: and he received sight forthwith, and arose, and was baptized.*

¹⁹ *And when he had received meat, he was strengthened. Then was Saul certain days with the disciples which were at Damascus.*

²⁰ *<u>And straightway he preached Christ in the synagogues, that he is the Son of God.</u>*

Acts 10:19-45

<u>¹⁹ While Peter thought on the vision, the Spirit said unto him, Behold, three men seek thee.</u>

<u>²⁰ Arise therefore, and get thee down, and go with them, doubting nothing: for I have sent them.</u>

<u>²¹ Then Peter went down to the men which were sent unto him from Cornelius; and said, Behold, I am he whom ye seek: what is the cause wherefore ye are come?</u>

<u>²² And they said, Cornelius the centurion, a just man, and one that feareth God, and of good report among all the nation of the Jews, was warned from God by an holy angel to send for thee into his house, and to hear words of thee.</u>

²³ Then called he them in, and lodged them. And on the morrow Peter went away with them, and certain brethren from Joppa accompanied him.

²⁴ And the morrow after they entered into Caesarea. And Cornelius waited for them, and he had called together his kinsmen and near friends.

²⁵ And as Peter was coming in, Cornelius met him, and fell down at his feet, and worshipped him.

²⁶ But Peter took him up, saying, Stand up; I myself also am a man.

²⁷ And as he talked with him, he went in, and found many that were come together.

²⁸ And he said unto them, Ye know how that it is an unlawful thing for a man that is a Jew to keep company, or come unto one of another nation; but God hath shewed me that I should not call any man common or unclean.

²⁹ *Therefore came I unto you without gainsaying, as soon as I was sent for: I ask therefore for what intent ye have sent for me?*

³⁰ *And Cornelius said, Four days ago I was fasting until this hour; and at the ninth hour I prayed in my house, and, behold, a man stood before me in bright clothing,*

³¹ *And said, Cornelius, thy prayer is heard, and thine alms are had in remembrance in the sight of God.*

³² *Send therefore to Joppa, and call hither Simon, whose surname is Peter; he is lodged in the house of one Simon a tanner by the sea side: who, when he cometh, shall speak unto thee.*

³³ *Immediately therefore I sent to thee; and thou hast well done that thou art come. Now therefore are we all here present before God, to hear all things that are commanded thee of God.*

³⁴ *Then Peter opened his mouth, and said, Of a truth I perceive that God is no respecter of persons:*

³⁵ *But in every nation he that feareth him, and worketh righteousness, is accepted with him.*

³⁶ *The word which God sent unto the children of Israel, preaching peace by Jesus Christ: (he is Lord of all:)*

³⁷ *That word, I say, ye know, which was published throughout all Judaea, and began from Galilee, after the baptism which John preached;*

³⁸ *How God anointed Jesus of Nazareth with the Holy Ghost and with power: who went about doing good, and healing all that were oppressed of the devil; for God was with him.*

³⁹ *And we are witnesses of all things which he did both in the land of the Jews, and in Jerusalem; whom they slew and hanged on a tree:*

<u>⁴⁰ Him God raised up the third day, and shewed him openly;</u>

⁴¹ *Not to all the people, but unto witnesses chosen before God, even to us, who did eat and drink with him after he rose from the dead.*

⁴² <u>*And he commanded us to preach unto the people,*</u> *and to testify that it is he which was ordained of God to be the Judge of quick and dead.*

⁴³ *To him give all the prophets witness, that through his name whosoever believeth in him shall receive remission of sins.*

⁴⁴ <u>*While Peter yet spake these words, the Holy Ghost fell on all them which heard the word.*</u>

⁴⁵ *And they of the circumcision which believed were astonished, as many as came with Peter, because that on the Gentiles also was poured out the gift of the Holy Ghost.*

Are there any examples of the Rapture in the Bible? Yes, we have already mentioned the experience of John in Revelation 4 but there are four other accounts of individuals being raptured. The accounts of Enoch, Elijah, Jesus, and the two witnesses are described below:

Genesis 5:19-24 Enoch

¹⁹ *And Jared lived after he begat Enoch eight hundred years, and begat sons and daughters:*

²⁰ *And all the days of Jared were nine hundred sixty and two years: and he died.*

²¹ *And Enoch lived sixty and five years, and begat Methuselah:*

²² *And Enoch walked with God after he begat Methuselah three hundred years, and begat sons and daughters:*

²³ *And all the days of Enoch were three hundred sixty and five years:*

²⁴ <u>*And Enoch walked with God: and he was not; for God took him.*</u>

Hebrews 11:5 Enoch

⁵ *By faith Enoch was translated that he should not see death; and was not found, because God had translated him: for before his <u>translation </u>he had this testimony, that he pleased God.*

2 Kings 2:8-13 Elijah

⁸ *And Elijah took his mantle, and wrapped it together, and smote the waters, and they were divided hither and thither, so that they two went over on dry ground.*

⁹ *And it came to pass, when they were gone over, that Elijah said unto Elisha, Ask what I shall do for thee, before I be taken away from thee. And Elisha said, I pray thee, let a double portion of thy spirit be upon me.*

¹⁰ *And he said, Thou hast asked a hard thing: nevertheless, if thou see me when I am taken from thee, it shall be so unto thee; but if not, it shall not be so.*

¹¹ *And it came to pass, as they still went on, and talked, that, behold, there appeared a chariot of fire, and horses of fire, and parted them both asunder; and <u>Elijah went up by a whirlwind into heaven</u>.*

¹² *And Elisha saw it, and he cried, My father, my father, the chariot of Israel, and the horsemen thereof. And he saw him no more: and he took hold of his own clothes, and rent them in two pieces.*

¹³ He took up also the mantle of Elijah that fell from him, and went back, and stood by the bank of Jordan,

Acts 1:8-11 Jesus

⁸ But ye shall receive power, after that the Holy Ghost is come upon you: and ye shall be witnesses unto me both in Jerusalem, and in all Judaea, and in Samaria, and unto the uttermost part of the earth.

⁹ And when he had spoken these things, while they beheld, he was taken up; and a cloud received him out of their sight.

¹⁰ And while they looked steadfastly toward heaven as he went up, behold, two men stood by them in white apparel;

¹¹ Which also said, Ye men of Galilee, why stand ye gazing up into heaven? this same Jesus, which is taken up from you into heaven, shall so come in like manner as ye have seen him go into heaven.

Revelation 11:7-12 Two Witnesses

⁷ And when they shall have finished their testimony, the beast that ascendeth out of the bottomless pit shall make war against them, and shall overcome them, and kill them.

⁸ And their dead bodies shall lie in the street of the great city, which spiritually is called Sodom and Egypt, where also our Lord was crucified.

⁹ And they of the people and kindreds and tongues and nations shall see their dead bodies three days and an half, and shall not suffer their dead bodies to be put in graves.

¹⁰ And they that dwell upon the earth shall rejoice over them, and make merry, and shall send gifts one to another;

because these two prophets tormented them that dwelt on the earth.

11 And after three days and an half the spirit of life from God entered into them, and they stood upon their feet; and great fear fell upon them which saw them.

12 <u>And they heard a great voice from heaven saying unto them, Come up hither. And they ascended up to heaven in a cloud</u>; and their enemies beheld them.

QUESTION 2

Why is there a Rapture?

The purpose of the Rapture is to provide God's people an escape from the wrath of God which he has appointed for the end of the days. This escape is similar to that provided Noah and his family at the time of the great flood and Lot and his family prior to the destruction of Sodom and Gomorrah.

Revelation 3: 7-10

⁷ And to the angel of the church in Philadelphia write; These things saith he that is holy, he that is true, he that hath the key of David, he that openeth, and no man shutteth; and shutteth, and no man openeth;

⁸ I know thy works: behold, I have set before thee an open door, and no man can shut it: for thou hast a little strength, and hast kept my word, and hast not denied my name.

⁹ Behold, I will make them of the synagogue of Satan, which say they are Jews, and are not, but do lie; behold, I will make them to come and worship before thy feet, and to know that I have loved thee. (See 1John 2:19; those who say they are believers and are not. The word Jew is used in the same way that John uses the word angel)

[10] Because thou hast kept the word of my patience, <u>I also will keep thee from the hour of temptation, which shall come upon all the world, to try them that dwell upon the earth.</u>

1Thessalonians 1:10 and 5:1-9

[10] And to wait for his Son from heaven, whom he raised from the dead, even Jesus, which delivered us from the wrath to come.

5 But of the times and the seasons, brethren, ye have no need that I write unto you.

[2] For yourselves know perfectly that the day of the Lord so cometh as a thief in the night.

[3] <u>For when they shall say, Peace and safety; then sudden destruction cometh upon them, as travail upon a woman with child; and they shall not escape.</u>

[4]<u>But ye, brethren, are not in darkness, that that day should overtake you as a thief.</u>

[5] Ye are all the children of light, and the children of the day: we are not of the night, nor of darkness.

[6] Therefore let us not sleep, as do others; but let us watch and be sober.

[7] For they that sleep sleep in the night; and they that be drunken are drunken in the night.

[8] But let us, who are of the day, be sober, putting on the breastplate of faith and love; and for an helmet, the hope of salvation.

⁹ For God hath not appointed us to wrath, but to obtain salvation by our Lord Jesus Christ,

Let's take a look at conditions on the earth in the days of Noah to determine why it was necessary to flood the earth and kill every living thing other than those who escaped in the ark. Gen 6 answers those questions. It states in verse 5 that God saw that the wickedness of man was great and all of his thoughts were evil. Verses 11 and 12 add that the earth was corrupt and filled with violence. These are indictments in general but it seems that the more specific reason for the judgment is contained in verses 1-4. They indicate that there were angels or giants on the earth that saw that women were beautiful and took them to be their wives. The resulting children were mighty and men of renown. The conclusion that can be made is that the angels, referred to as Sons of God in verse 2, were breeding a super race which was contrary to God's plan. God then destroyed the human race except for the family of Noah which was then used to repopulate the world.

Genesis 6

6 And it came to pass, when men began to multiply on the face of the earth, and daughters were born unto them,
² That the sons of God saw the daughters of men that they were fair; and they took them wives of all which they chose.
³ And the LORD said, My spirit shall not always strive with man, for that he also is flesh: yet his days shall be an hundred and twenty years.
⁴ There were giants in the earth in those days; and also after that, when the sons of God came in unto the daughters of men,

<u>and they bare children to them, the same became mighty men which were of old, men of renown.</u>

⁵ <u>And God saw that the wickedness of man was great in the earth, and that every imagination of the thoughts of his heart was only evil continually</u>.

⁶ And it repented the L<small>ORD</small> that he had made man on the earth, and it grieved him at his heart.

⁷ <u>And the L</u><small><u>ORD</u></small> <u>said, I will destroy man whom I have created from the face of the earth; both man, and beast, and the creeping thing, and the fowls of the air</u>; for it repenteth me that I have made them.

⁸ But <u>Noah found grace in the eyes of the L</u><small><u>ORD</u></small><u>.</u>

⁹ These are the generations of Noah: Noah was a just man and perfect in his generations, and Noah walked with God.

¹⁰ And Noah begat three sons, Shem, Ham, and Japheth.

¹¹ The earth also was corrupt before God, and the earth was filled with violence.

¹² <u>And God looked upon the earth, and, behold, it was corrupt; for all flesh had corrupted his way upon the earth.</u>

¹³ <u>And God said unto Noah, The end of all flesh is come before me; for the earth is filled with violence through them; and, behold, I will destroy them with the earth.</u>

¹⁴ Make thee an ark of gopher wood; rooms shalt thou make in the ark, and shalt pitch it within and without with pitch.

¹⁵ And this is the fashion which thou shalt make it of: The length of the ark shall be three hundred cubits, the breadth of it fifty cubits, and the height of it thirty cubits.

¹⁶ A window shalt thou make to the ark, and in a cubit shalt thou finish it above; and the door of the ark shalt thou set in the side thereof; with lower, second, and third stories shalt thou make it.

17 And, behold, I, even I, do bring a flood of waters upon the earth, to destroy all flesh, wherein is the breath of life, from under heaven; and every thing that is in the earth shall die.

18 But with thee will I establish my covenant; and thou shalt come into the ark, thou, and thy sons, and thy wife, and thy sons' wives with thee.

19 And of every living thing of all flesh, two of every sort shalt thou bring into the ark, to keep them alive with thee; they shall be male and female.

20 Of fowls after their kind, and of cattle after their kind, of every creeping thing of the earth after his kind, two of every sort shall come unto thee, to keep them alive.

21 And take thou unto thee of all food that is eaten, and thou shalt gather it to thee; and it shall be for food for thee, and for them.

22 Thus did Noah; according to all that God commanded him, so did he.

There is another book that may add to the information in Gen 6. It is the <u>Book of Enoch</u> and it <u>is not Scripture</u>. It should not be given the same weight as scripture. It can be considered as commentary. Chapters 7-10 are interesting and are reproduced below. In summary, Chapter 7 below confirms Gen 6 that angels admired the daughters of men and took them for their wives. The women conceived and brought forth giants. The angels were evil and turned against man and beast. Chapter 8 tells how evil practices progressed. Then, in Chapter 9, some of the angels in heaven, including Michael and Gabriel, appealed to God to do something about the conditions on the earth. Their main complaint seems to be that the human race had become polluted. In Chapter 10 God responds by sending a messenger to the son of Lamech, telling him how he and his family can escape the coming flood. Lamech is identified as the father of Noah in Gen 5:28 and 29.

One conclusion that can be made from the book of Enoch is that God destroyed the human race, except for Noah and his family, to prevent Satan from polluting the gene pool of humanity and drastically changing God's plan.

Satan will be equally intent on preventing the rapture and resurrection of His saints prior to delivering His wrath upon the earth. This time He will not destroy the earth. He will deliver His wrath upon the antichrist until he evicts him and takes rightful possession of the earth. We will rule with him as kings and priests.

Book of Enoch Chapter 7

(THIS IS NOT SCRIPTURE)

1It happened after the sons of men had multiplied in those days, that daughters were born to them, elegant and beautiful.

2And when the angels, **(3)** the sons of heaven, beheld them, they became enamoured of them, saying to each other, Come, let us select for ourselves wives from the progeny of men, and let us beget children.

(3) An Aramaic text reads "Watchers" here (J.T. Milik, *Aramaic Fragments of Qumran Cave 4* [Oxford: Clarendon Press, 1976], p. 167).

3Then their leader Samyaza said to them; I fear that you may perhaps be indisposed to the performance of this enterprise;

4And that I alone shall suffer for so grievous a crime.

5But they answered him and said; We all swear,

6And bind ourselves by mutual execrations, that we will not change our intention, but execute our projected undertaking.

7Then they swore all together, and all bound themselves by mutual execrations. Their whole number was two hundred, who descended upon Ardis, **(4)** which is the top of mount Armon.

(4) **Upon Ardis.** Or, «in the days of Jared» (R.H. Charles, ed. and trans., *The Book of Enoch* [Oxford: Clarendon Press, 1893], p. 63).

8That mountain therefore was called Armon, because they had sworn upon it, **(5)** and bound themselves by mutual execrations.

(5) Mt. Armon, or Mt. Hermon, derives its name from the Hebrew word *herem*, a curse (Charles, p. 63).

9These are the names of their chiefs: Samyaza, who was their leader, Urakabarameel, Akibeel, Tamiel, Ramuel, Danel, Azkeel, Saraknyal, Asael, Armers, Batraal, Anane, Zavebe, Samsaveel, Ertael, Turel, Yomyael, Arazyal. These were the prefects of the two hundred angels, and the remainder were all with them. **(6)**

(6) The Aramaic texts preserve an earlier list of names of these Watchers: Semihazah; Artqoph; Ramtel; Kokabel; Ramel; Danieal; Zeqiel; Baraqel; Asael;

Hermoni; Matarel; Ananel; Stawel; Samsiel; Sahriel; Tummiel; Turiel; Yomiel; Yhaddiel (Milik, p. 151).

10Then they took wives, each choosing for himself; whom they began to approach, and with whom they cohabited; teaching them sorcery, incantations, and the dividing of roots and trees.

11And the women conceiving brought forth giants, **(7)**

(7) The Greek texts vary considerably from the Ethiopic text here. One Greek manuscript adds to this section, "And they [the women] bore to them [the Watchers] three races–first, the great giants. The giants brought forth [some say "slew"] the Naphelim, and the Naphelim brought forth [or "slew"] the Elioud. And they existed, increasing in power according to their greatness." See the account in the Book of Jubilees.

12Whose stature was each three hundred cubits. These devoured all *which* the labor of men *produced;* until it became impossible to feed them;

13When they turned themselves against men, in order to devour them;

14And began to injure birds, beasts, reptiles, and fishes, to eat their flesh one after another, **(8)** and to drink their blood.

(8) **Their flesh one after another.** Or, «one another's flesh.» R.H. Charles notes that this phrase may refer

to the destruction of one class of giants by another (Charles, p. 65).

15Then the earth reproved the unrighteous.

Chapter 8

1Moreover Azazyel taught men to make swords, knives, shields, breastplates, the fabrication of mirrors, and the workmanship of bracelets and ornaments, the use of paint, the beautifying of the eyebrows, *the use of* stones of every valuable and select kind, and all sorts of dyes, so that the world became altered.

2Impiety increased; fornication multiplied; and they transgressed and corrupted all their ways.

3Amazarak taught all the sorcerers, and dividers of roots:

4Armers *taught* the solution of sorcery;

5Barkayal *taught* the observers of the stars, **(9)**

(9) **Observers of the stars.** Astrologers (Charles, p. 67).

6Akibeel *taught* signs;

7Tamiel taught astronomy;

8And Asaradel taught the motion of the moon,

9And men, being destroyed, cried out; and their voice reached to heaven.

Chapter 9

1Then Michael and Gabriel, Raphael, Suryal, and Uriel, looked down from heaven, and saw the quantity of blood which was shed on earth, and all the iniquity which was done upon it, and said one to another, *It is* the voice of their cries;

2The earth deprived *of her children* has cried even to the gate of heaven.

3And now to you, O you holy one of heaven, the souls of men complain, saying, Obtain Justice for us with **(10)** the Most High. Then they said to their Lord, the King, *You are* Lord of lords, God of gods, King of kings. The throne of your glory is for ever and ever, and for ever and ever is your name sanctified and glorified. You are blessed and glorified.

(10) **Obtain justice for us with.** Literally, «Bring judgment to us from.» (Richard Laurence, ed. and trans., *The Book of Enoch the Prophet* [London: Kegan Paul, Trench & Co., 1883], p. 9).

4You have made all things; you possess power over all things; and all things are open and manifest before you. You behold all things, and nothing can be concealed from you.

5You have seen what Azazyel has done, how he has taught every species of iniquity upon earth, and has disclosed to the world all the secret things which are done in the heavens.

6Samyaza also has taught sorcery, to whom you have given authority over those who are associated with him. They have gone together to the daughters of men; have lain with them; have become polluted;

7And have discovered crimes **(11)** to them.

(11) **Discovered crimes.** Or, «revealed these sins» (Charles, p. 70).

8The women likewise have brought forth giants.

9Thus has the whole earth been filled with blood and with iniquity.

10And now behold the souls of those who are dead, cry out.

11And complain even to the gate of heaven.

12Their groaning ascends; nor can they escape from the unrighteousness which is committed on earth. You know all things, before they exist.

13You know these things, and what has been done by them; yet you do not speak to us.

14What on account of these things ought we to do to them?

Chapter 10

1Then the Most High, the Great and Holy One spoke,

2And sent Arsayalalyur **(12)** to the son of Lamech,

(12) **Arsayalalyur.** Here one Greek text reads «Uriel.»

3Saying, Say to him in my name, Conceal yourself.

4Then explain to him the consummation which is about to take place; for all the earth shall perish; the waters of a deluge shall come over the whole earth, and all things which are in it shall be destroyed.

5And now teach him how he may escape, and how his seed may remain in all the earth.

6Again the Lord said to Raphael, Bind Azazyel hand and foot; cast him into darkness; and opening the desert which is in Dudael, cast him in there.

7Throw upon him hurled and pointed stones, covering him with darkness;

8There shall he remain for ever; cover his face, that he may not see the light.

9And in the great day of judgment let him be cast into the fire.

10Restore the earth, which the angels have corrupted; and announce life to it, that I may revive it.

11All the sons of men shall not perish in consequence of every secret, by which the Watchers have destroyed, and *which* they have taught, their offspring.

12All the earth has been corrupted by the effects of the teaching of Azazyel. To him therefore ascribe the whole crime.

13To Gabriel also the Lord said, Go to the biters, **(13)** to the reprobates, to the children of fornication; and destroy the children of fornication, the offspring of the Watchers, from among men; bring them forth, and excite them one against another. Let them perish by *mutual* slaughter; for length of days shall not be theirs.

(13) **Biters.** More accurately, «bastards» (Charles, p. 73; Michael A. Knibb, ed. and trans., *The Ethiopic Book of Enoch* [Oxford: Clarendon Press, 1978], p. 88).

14They shall all entreat you, but their fathers shall not obtain *their wishes* respecting them; for they shall hope for eternal life, and that they may live, each of them, five hundred years.

15To Michael likewise the Lord said, Go and announce *his crime* to Samyaza, and to the others who are with him, who have been associated with women, that they might be polluted with all their impurity. And when all their sons shall be slain, when they shall see the perdition of their beloved, bind them for seventy generations underneath the earth, even to the day of judgment, and of consummation, until the judgment, *the effect of* which will last for ever, be completed.

16Then shall they be taken away into the lowest depths of the fire in torments; and in confinement shall they be shut up for ever.

17Immediately after this shall he, **(14)** together with them, burn and perish; they shall be bound until the consummation of many generations.

(14) **He.** I.e., Samyaza.

18Destroy all the souls addicted to dalliance, **(15)** and the offspring of the Watchers, for they have tyrannized over mankind.

(15) **Dalliance.** Or, «lust» (Knibb, p. 90; cp. Charles, p. 76).

19Let every oppressor perish from the face of the earth;
20Let every evil work be destroyed;
21The plant of righteousness and of rectitude appear, and its produce become a blessing.

22Righteousness and rectitude shall be for ever planted with delight.

23And then shall all the saints give thanks, and live until they have begotten a thousand *children*, while the whole period of their youth, and their sabbaths shall be completed in peace. In those days all the earth shall be cultivated in righteousness; it shall be wholly planted with trees, and filled with benediction; every tree of delight shall be planted in it.

24In it shall vines be planted; and the vine which shall be planted in it shall yield fruit to satiety; every seed, which shall be sown in it, shall produce for one measure a thousand; and one measure of olives shall produce ten presses of oil.

25Purify the earth from all oppression, from all injustice, from all crime, from all impiety, and from all the pollution which is committed upon it. Exterminate them from the earth.

26Then shall all the children of men be righteous, and all nations shall pay me divine honours, and bless me; and all shall adore me.

27The earth shall be cleansed from all corruption, from every crime, from all punishment, and from all suffering; neither will I again send a deluge upon it from generation to generation for ever.

28In those days I will open the treasures of blessing which are in heaven, that I may cause them to descend upon earth, and upon all the works and labour of man.

29Peace and equity shall associate with the sons of men all the days of the world, in every generation of it.

QUESTION 3

When is the Rapture?

This is a more difficult question to answer. There are three common schools of thought regarding the timing of the Rapture. As you can see from the answer to the second question, "Why is there a Rapture?", I believe that the Rapture occurs prior to the wrath of God or tribulation that comes upon the earth at the end of the days. There is another school of thought that says that the Rapture occurs in the midst of the wrath or tribulation period. A final school of thought says that the Rapture occurs near the end of the tribulation period.

I believe the pre-wrath or pre-tribulation Rapture school of thought is correct and will cite scripture in support of that position. Please bear with me as we review verses in Matthew 24 (Olivet Discourse), Daniel 7, and Revelation 4-7. Arthur E. Bloomfield wrote extensively regarding Daniel, Revelation, and the Olivet Discourse. His work has greatly influenced my thinking and I recommend that you read some of his books.

Information from all three sources is necessary to determine when the Rapture will occur. We will not be determining the day or the hour of the Rapture but by knowing the times and seasons we can determine a sequence of events and put them into the timeframe designated by Jesus in the Olivet Discourse.

Let's start by reviewing Matthew 24.

Matthew 24:3-14

³ And as he sat upon the mount of Olives, the disciples came unto him privately, saying, Tell us, when shall these things be? and what shall be the sign of thy coming, and of the end of the world?

⁴ And Jesus answered and said unto them, Take heed that no man deceive you.

⁵ For many shall come in my name, saying, I am Christ; and shall deceive many.

⁶ And ye shall hear of wars and rumours of wars: see that ye be not troubled: <u>for all these things must come to pass, but the end is not yet.</u> (the Rapture follows v.6 and v.7-14 are the persecution of the left behind saints)

⁷ For nation shall rise against nation, and kingdom against kingdom: and there shall be famines, and pestilences, and earthquakes, in divers places.

⁸ All these are the beginning of sorrows.

⁹ Then shall they deliver you up to be afflicted, and shall kill you: and ye shall be hated of all nations for my name's sake. (same as Rev 6:9-11, 7:9-15, 15:2, Dan 7:21 and 25)

¹⁰ And then shall many be offended, and shall betray one another, and shall hate one another.

[11] And many false prophets shall rise, and shall deceive many.

[12] And because iniquity shall abound, the love of many shall wax cold.

[13] But he that shall endure unto the end, the same shall be saved.

[14] <u>And this gospel of the kingdom shall be preached in all the world for a witness unto all nations; and then shall the end come.</u>

In verse 3 above the disciples ask Jesus what will be the sign of His coming and of the end of the world (end of the age). Jesus partially answers their questions in verses 4-6. He tells them not to be deceived by the many who will claim that they are Christ and that they will hear of wars and rumors of wars. Then he tells them at the end of verse 6 that these things must come to pass "but the end is not yet." Those words indicate that the signs precede the beginning of the end and once they have happened we can expect the commencement of the end of the days to start. Mark and Luke have parallel accounts of the Olivet Discourse and Luke adds one important detail.

Luke 21:28

[28] And when these things begin to come to pass, then look up, and lift up your heads; for your redemption draweth nigh.

We are to be watchful for the signs and when we see them we know that our redemption is near. Our redemption in this case is the Rapture. It is the point in time when true believers, Gods own people, are redeemed from the fallen world and are saved from the wrath or tribulation which will come upon the world. The Rapture occurs between verse 6 and 7. The amount of time between verse 6 and 7 is not known. Then in verse 7 the tribulation or wrath starts. Verses 7-14 describe the events which are the beginning of the end of the age. It appears that many things happen at once. Verse 7 declares that there will be wars, famines, pestilences, and earthquakes, all in divers places on the earth. Chapters 5 and 6 in the book of Revelation describe the same events that occur in verses 7-14 of Mat 24. Before we get to Revelation 5 and 6 we must first start at chapter 4 in Revelation and proceed from there.

Revelation 4:1-6

4 After this I looked, and, behold, a door was opened in heaven: and the first voice which I heard was as it were of a trumpet talking with me; which said, Come up hither, and I will shew thee things which must be hereafter. (the Rapture)

² And immediately I was in the spirit: and, behold, a throne was set in heaven, and one sat on the throne.

³ And he that sat was to look upon like a jasper and a sardine stone: and there was a rainbow round about the throne, in sight like unto an emerald.

⁴ And round about the throne were four and twenty seats: and upon the seats I saw four and twenty elders sitting, clothed in white raiment; and they had on their heads crowns of gold. (attire of saints)

⁵ And out of the throne proceeded lightnings and thunderings and voices: and there were seven lamps of fire burning before the throne, which are the seven Spirits of God.

⁶ And before the throne there was a <u>sea of glass</u> like unto crystal: and in the midst of the throne, and round about the throne, were four beasts full of eyes before and behind.

In this passage John has a vision of being raptured to heaven and the scene is around the throne of God. John is not alone. Around the throne there are twenty-four elders dressed in white, four beasts full of eyes, and all around the throne there was a sea of glass. As already mentioned, the sea is descriptive of large numbers or multitudes of people. Verses 8-11 of Rev 5 identify the vast number of people.

Now that it has been established, at least for some of us, that the Rapture has occurred by the events described in Rev 4, we can now turn to Rev 5 and 6.

Revelation 5

5 And I saw in the right hand of him that sat on the throne a book written within and on the backside, sealed with seven seals. (title deed to the earth)

² And I saw a strong angel proclaiming with a loud voice, Who is worthy to open the book, and to loose the seals thereof?

³ And no man in heaven, nor in earth, neither under the earth, was able to open the book, neither to look thereon.

⁴ And I wept much, because no man was found worthy to open and to read the book, neither to look thereon.

⁵ And one of the elders saith unto me, Weep not: behold, the Lion of the tribe of Judah, the Root of David, hath prevailed to open the book, and to loose the seven seals thereof. (Jesus opened the book)

⁶ And I beheld, and, lo, in the midst of the throne and of the four beasts, and in the midst of the elders, stood a Lamb as it had been slain, having seven horns and seven eyes, which are the seven Spirits of God sent forth into all the earth.

⁷ And he came and took the book out of the right hand of him that sat upon the throne. (Jesus and God the Father)

⁸ And when he had taken the book, the four beasts and four and twenty elders fell down before the Lamb, having every one of them harps, and golden vials full of odours, which are the prayers of saints.

⁹ And they sung a new song, saying, Thou art worthy to take the book, and to open the seals thereof: for thou wast slain, and hast redeemed us to God by thy blood out of every kindred, and tongue, and people, and nation; (angels cannot sing this song)

¹⁰ And hast made us unto our God kings and priests: and we shall reign on the earth. (this has to be more than 24 elders)

¹¹ And I beheld, and I heard the voice of many angels round about the throne and the beasts and the elders: and the number of them was ten thousand times ten thousand, and thousands of thousands;

¹² Saying with a loud voice, Worthy is the Lamb that was slain to receive power, and riches, and wisdom, and strength, and honour, and glory, and blessing.

¹³ And every creature which is in heaven, and on the earth, and under the earth, and such as are in the sea, and all that are in them, heard I saying, Blessing, and honour, and glory, and power, be unto him that sitteth upon the throne, and unto the Lamb for ever and ever.

¹⁴ And the four beasts said, Amen. And the four and twenty elders fell down and worshipped him that liveth for ever and ever.

The book in verse 1 above, as already mentioned, is the title deed to the earth. Opening the seals starts the redemption of all that was lost in the garden in the book of Genesis. God gave Adam dominion over the earth in Gen 1:26 but Adam lost that dominion because of his sin. In Gen 3:14 and 15 God is speaking to the serpent who tempted Eve and here is what was said: *14 And the LORD God said unto the serpent, Because thou hast done this, thou art cursed above all cattle, and above every beast of the field; upon thy belly shalt thou go, and dust shalt thou eat all the days of thy life: 15 And I will put enmity between thee and the woman, and between thy seed and her seed; it shall bruise thy head, and thou shalt bruise his heel.* The imagery here is that the serpent is creeping along the ground and bites or bruises the heel of the seed of the woman. Jesus is the seed of the woman and he bruises the head of the serpent. This is a prophetic verse that looks forward to the redemption of man and the earth. Jesus has already paid the blood price to redeem mankind and now in verse 1 of Rev 5 above it is Jesus who is starting the process that will evict Satan and physically return to earth to reclaim it as the rightful owner. In Rev 6 He begins opening the seals to start the process of redemption of the earth.

Revelation 6

6 And I saw when the <u>Lamb opened one of the seals</u>, and I heard, as it were the noise of thunder, one of the four beasts saying, Come and see.

2 And I saw, and behold a white horse: and he that sat on him had a bow; and a crown was given unto him: and he went forth conquering, and to conquer. (preaching the gospel)

3 And when he had opened the <u>second seal</u>, I heard the second beast say, Come and see.

⁴ And there went out another horse that was red: and power was given to him that sat thereon to take peace from the earth, and that they should kill one another: and there was given unto him a great sword.

⁵ And when he had opened the <u>third seal</u>, I heard the third beast say, Come and see. And I beheld, and lo a black horse; and he that sat on him had a pair of balances in his hand.

⁶ And I heard a voice in the midst of the four beasts say, A measure of wheat for a penny, and three measures of barley for a penny; and see thou hurt not the oil and the wine. (food distribution)

⁷ And when he had opened the <u>fourth seal</u>, I heard the voice of the fourth beast say, Come and see.

⁸ And I looked, and behold a pale horse: and his name that sat on him was Death, and Hell followed with him. And power was given unto them over the <u>fourth part of the earth, to kill with sword</u>, and with hunger, and with death, and with the beasts of the earth. (1/4 of population killed, then in Rev 9:18 1/3 of remaining population killed, that means that ½ of world population will be killed during the tribulation for the left behind saints and the 7-year tribulation for Israel)

⁹ And when he had opened the fifth seal, <u>I saw under the altar the souls of them that were slain for the word of God, and for the testimony which they held</u>: (tribulation saints)

¹⁰ And they cried with a loud voice, saying, How long, O Lord, holy and true, dost thou not judge and avenge our blood on them that dwell on the earth?

¹¹ And <u>white robes were given unto every one of them; and it was said unto them, that they should rest yet for a little season, until their fellowservants also and their brethren, that should be</u>

killed as they were, should be fulfilled. (clothing of the saints) (42 months per Rev 12:14 and Dan 7:25)

¹² And I beheld when he had opened the <u>sixth seal</u>, and, lo, there was a great earthquake; and the sun became black as sackcloth of hair, and the moon became as blood;

¹³ And the stars of heaven fell unto the earth, even as a fig tree casteth her untimely figs, when she is shaken of a mighty wind.

¹⁴ And the heaven departed as a scroll when it is rolled together; and every mountain and island were moved out of their places.

¹⁵ And the kings of the earth, and the great men, and the rich men, and the chief captains, and the mighty men, and every bondman, and every free man, hid themselves in the dens and in the rocks of the mountains;

¹⁶ And said to the mountains and rocks, Fall on us, and hide us from the face of him that sitteth on the throne, and from the wrath of the Lamb:

¹⁷ For the great day of his wrath is come; and who shall be able to stand?

The opening of the seals on what appears to be the title deed to the earth is what starts the pouring out of God's wrath upon the earth in preparation to take rightful possession. John and the rest of the raptured saints are in heaven because they witness the Lamb opening the seals, one at a time. This supports the pre-tribulation position. When the Lamb opened the second, third, and fourth seals peace was taken from the earth followed by death and famine. This is essentially what happens in verse 7 of Matthew 24 so both Matthew 24 and Revelation are describing the same event. They are both describing the events that happen immediately after the Rapture. Matthew 24:8 states further that "all these are the beginning of sorrows."

The first seal opened by the lamb is the most difficult to understand. When the Lamb opened it He sent forth a rider on a white horse carrying a bow to go forth to conquer. Most commentaries say that this is some type of warrior or even the antichrist. One has to ask, why would Jesus, the Lamb, send forth the antichrist or why did the rider not have any arrows if he was a warrior? In researching the use of the bow in the Bible we find that there are two places where it is used in a different sense than as a tool of war. In Gen 9:13-16 the bow was used by God as an oath and in Habakkuk 3:9 the bow was referred to as an oath "thy word".

Genesis 9:12-17

¹² And God said, This is the token of the covenant which I make between me and you and every living creature that is with you, for perpetual generations:

¹³ I do set my bow in the cloud, and it shall be for a token of a covenant between me and the earth.

¹⁴ And it shall come to pass, when I bring a cloud over the earth, that the bow shall be seen in the cloud:

¹⁵ And I will remember my covenant, which is between me and you and every living creature of all flesh; and the waters shall no more become a flood to destroy all flesh.

¹⁶ And the bow shall be in the cloud; and I will look upon it, that I may remember the everlasting covenant between God and every living creature of all flesh that is upon the earth.

¹⁷ <u>And God said unto Noah, This is the token of the covenant, which I have established between me and all flesh that is upon the earth.</u>

Habakkuk 3:9

⁹ Thy bow was made quite naked, <u>according to the oaths of the tribes, even thy word.</u> Selah. Thou didst cleave the earth with rivers.

There is a commentary written by John Gill, commenting on the reference to the bow in Hab 3:9 in which he states "the bow is an emblem of the Gospel, with which Christ, the Captain of our salvation, …..went forth, especially in the first stages of Christianity, conquering and to conquer." The bow is the Word of God and is the means by which people are saved. With that we can conclude that the rider on the white horse is not a warrior but is preaching the word of God. So, <u>after</u> the Rapture, the Gospel is "preached in all the world, for a witness unto all nations". Many will be saved through this preaching and many of these tribulation saints will be delivered up to be afflicted, persecuted, hated, and killed.

Matthew 24:14 and 9

¹⁴ And this gospel of the kingdom shall be preached in all the world for a witness unto all nations; and then shall the end come.

⁹ Then shall they deliver you up to be afflicted, and shall kill you: and ye shall be hated of all nations for my name's sake.

The preaching of the Gospel unto all nations in verse 14 above is known as the latter rain. Note that it happens after the rapture but prior to the end of the world. The end of the world is really the end of the Church age. The former and latter rain are identified in Joel 2:28-32 and is quoted by Peter in Acts 2.

Joel 2:28-32

28 And it shall come to pass afterward, that I will pour out my spirit upon all flesh; and your sons and your daughters shall prophesy, your old men shall dream dreams, your young men shall see visions:

29 And also upon the servants and upon the handmaids in those days will I pour out my spirit.

30 And I will shew wonders in the heavens and in the earth, blood, and fire, and pillars of smoke.

31 The sun shall be turned into darkness, and the moon into blood, before the great and terrible day of the LORD come.

32 And it shall come to pass, that whosoever shall call on the name of the LORD shall be delivered: for in mount Zion and in Jerusalem shall be deliverance, as the LORD hath said, and in the remnant whom the LORD shall call.

Verses 28 and 29 are the former rain and happened on the day of Pentecost. They were quoted by Peter in his sermon describing the events that occurred during the assembly of followers of Jesus in Jerusalem. The former rain marks the birth of the church and is known as the day of Pentecost. Peter also quoted verses 30 and 31 but a review of those verses indicates that those events have not yet happened. When they do happen Mat 24:14, the latter rain, will be fulfilled. This event is also described in Rev 14 and I have already discussed it in Chapter 1 of this book. Here is the part of Acts 2 that includes Peter's sermon:

Acts 2

And when the day of Pentecost was fully come, they were all with one accord in one place.

² And suddenly there came a sound from heaven as of a rushing mighty wind, and it filled all the house where they were sitting.

³ And there appeared unto them cloven tongues like as of fire, and it sat upon each of them.

⁴ And they were all filled with the Holy Ghost, and began to speak with other tongues, as the Spirit gave them utterance.

¹² And they were all amazed, and were in doubt, saying one to another, What meaneth this?

¹³ Others mocking said, These men are full of new wine.

¹⁴ But Peter, standing up with the eleven, lifted up his voice, and said unto them, Ye men of Judaea, and all ye that dwell at Jerusalem, be this known unto you, and hearken to my words:

¹⁵ For these are not drunken, as ye suppose, seeing it is but the third hour of the day.

¹⁶ But this is that which was spoken by the prophet Joel;

¹⁷ And it shall come to pass in the last days, saith God, I will pour out of my Spirit upon all flesh: and your sons and your daughters shall prophesy, and your young men shall see visions, and your old men shall dream dreams:

¹⁸ And on my servants and on my handmaidens I will pour out in those days of my Spirit; and they shall prophesy:

<u>¹⁹ *And I will shew wonders in heaven above, and signs in the earth beneath; blood, and fire, and vapour of smoke:*</u>

<u>²⁰ *The sun shall be turned into darkness, and the moon into blood, before the great and notable day of the Lord come:*</u>

<u>²¹ *And it shall come to pass, that whosoever shall call on the name of the Lord shall be saved.*</u>

Rev 6:9-11 above describes the killing of the tribulation saints mentioned in Mat 24:9 above.

In Rev 7, starting in verse 9, we see the whole number of tribulation saints in their white robes in a worship service around the throne. Again, this is after the Rapture because the raptured saints witness the event.

Revelation 7:9-15

⁹ *After this I beheld, and, lo, a great multitude, which no man could number, of all nations, and kindreds, and people, and tongues, stood before the throne, and before the Lamb, clothed with white robes, and palms in their hands;* (tribulation Saints join raptured and resurrected Saints around the throne, the sea of glass now complete. Angels are not part of this celebration because they are not part of the church)

¹⁰ *And cried with a loud voice, saying, Salvation to our God which sitteth upon the throne, and unto the Lamb.* (voices of the saints)

¹¹ *And all the angels stood round about the throne, and about the elders and the four beasts, and fell before the throne on their faces, and worshipped God,*

¹² *Saying, Amen: Blessing, and glory, and wisdom, and thanksgiving, and honour, and power, and might, be unto our God for ever and ever. Amen.*

13 And one of the elders answered, saying unto me, <u>What are these which are arrayed in white robes?</u> and whence came they?

14 And I said unto him, Sir, thou knowest. And he said to me, <u>These are they which came out of great tribulation, and have washed their robes, and made them white in the blood of the Lamb.</u>

15 Therefore are they before the throne of God, and serve him day and night in his temple: and he that sitteth on the throne shall dwell among them.

As already stated, Mat 24:14 says that the Gospel will be preached in all the world and then it concludes by saying "and then the end shall come."

The reference here is not to the return of Jesus with his saints to set up His Kingdom; it is to the end of the Church age. From the passages that we looked at in Matthew and Revelation we can conclude that there will be a group of believers that is raptured to heaven and they will be joined by another group of saints who became believers after the Rapture and lose their lives during a great persecution.

Jesus will return to earth accompanied by His saints at the end of a seven-year period commonly known as Daniels 70th week. At that time, He will set up His Kingdom and we will reign with Him as kings and priests as stated in Rev 5:10.

Before we move on to answer the fourth question it is important to determine how long the persecution of the tribulation saints will last. The Olivet Discourse in Matthew 24 does not give us any clues of its length but Revelation and Daniel do.

Daniel 7 describes world events at the time of the Rapture and for a short period of time after the Rapture.

Daniel 7

7 In the first year of Belshazzar king of Babylon Daniel had a dream and visions of his head upon his bed: then he wrote the dream, and told the sum of the matters.

²Daniel spake and said, I saw in my vision by night, and, behold, <u>the four winds of the heaven strove upon the great sea.</u>

³<u>And four great beasts came up from the sea</u>, diverse one from another.

⁴The first was like a <u>lion, and had eagle's wings</u>: I beheld till the wings thereof were plucked, and it was lifted up from the earth, and made stand upon the feet as a man, and a man's heart was given to it. (Babylon, head of gold)

⁵And behold another beast, <u>a second, like to a bear</u>, and it raised up itself on one side, and it had three ribs in the mouth of it between the teeth of it: and they said thus unto it, Arise, devour much flesh. (Medes/Persians, arms and chest of silver)

⁶After this I beheld, and lo another, <u>like a leopard</u>, which had upon the back of it four wings of a fowl; the beast had also four heads; and dominion was given to it. (Greece, belly and thighs of bronze)

⁷After this I saw in the night visions, and behold <u>a fourth beast</u>, dreadful and terrible, and strong exceedingly; and it had great iron teeth: it devoured and brake in pieces, and stamped the residue with the feet of it: and it was diverse from all the beasts that were before it; and it had ten horns. (Rome, legs of iron and feet of clay)

⁸ *I considered the horns, and, behold, <u>there came up among them another little horn</u>, before whom there were three of the first horns plucked up by the roots: and, behold, in this horn were eyes like the eyes of man, and a mouth speaking great things.* (rise of antichrist)

⁹ *I beheld till the thrones were cast down, and the Ancient of days did sit, whose garment was white as snow, and the hair of his head like the pure wool: his throne was like the fiery flame, and his wheels as burning fire.* (Rev 4)

¹⁰ *A fiery stream issued and came forth from before him: thousand thousands ministered unto him, and ten thousand times ten thousand stood before him: the judgment was set, and the books were opened.* (Rev 4)

¹¹ *I beheld then because of the voice of the great words which the horn spake: I beheld even till the beast was slain, and his body destroyed, and given to the burning flame.* (antichrist)

¹² *As concerning the rest of the beasts, they had their dominion taken away: yet their lives were prolonged for a season and time.*

¹³ *I saw in the night visions, and, behold, one like the Son of man came with the clouds of heaven, and came to the Ancient of days, and they brought him near before him.* (Jesus and God the Father)

¹⁴ *And there was given him dominion, and glory, and a kingdom, that all people, nations, and languages, should serve him: his dominion is an everlasting dominion, which shall not pass away, and his kingdom that which shall not be destroyed.* (kingdom is eternal)

¹⁵ *I Daniel was grieved in my spirit in the midst of my body, and the visions of my head troubled me.*

¹⁶ I came near unto one of them that stood by, and asked him the truth of all this. So he told me, and made me know the interpretation of the things.

¹⁷ These great beasts, which are four, are four kings, which shall arise out of the earth. (the great sea)

¹⁸ But the saints of the Most High shall take the kingdom, and possess the kingdom for ever, even for ever and ever. (the First Advent provided a means for eternal life through the death and resurrection of Jesus and during the Second Advent those who have been provided this salvation shall return with Jesus to possess the Kingdom) (Who are the saints? See v. 18 and 27., they return with Jesus in Rev 19. Which kingdom does the verse refer to? See v. 14 and 27, kingdom is eternal)

¹⁹ Then I would know the truth of the fourth beast, which was diverse from all the others, exceeding dreadful, whose teeth were of iron, and his nails of brass; which devoured, brake in pieces, and stamped the residue with his feet;

²⁰ And of the ten horns that were in his head, and of the other which came up, and before whom three fell; even of <u>that horn that had eyes, and a mouth that spake very great things, whose look was more stout than his fellows.</u> (antichrist described)

²¹ I beheld, and the same horn made war with the saints, and prevailed against them;

²² Until the Ancient of days came, and judgment was given to the saints of the most High; and the time came that the saints possessed the kingdom.

²³ Thus he said, The fourth beast shall be the fourth kingdom upon earth, which shall be diverse from all kingdoms, and shall

devour the whole earth, and shall tread it down, and break it in pieces.

²⁴ And the ten horns out of this kingdom are ten kings that shall arise: and another shall rise after them; and he shall be diverse from the first, and he shall subdue three kings.

²⁵ And he shall speak great words against the most High, and shall wear out the saints of the Most High, and think to change times and laws: and they shall be given into his hand until a time and times and the dividing of time. (persecution lasts 42 months)

²⁶ But the judgment shall sit, and they shall take away his dominion, to consume and to destroy it unto the end.

²⁷ And the kingdom and dominion, and the greatness of the kingdom under the whole heaven, shall be given to the people of the saints of the Most High, whose kingdom is an everlasting kingdom, and all dominions shall serve and obey him. (victory!!)

²⁸ Hitherto is the end of the matter. As for me Daniel, my cogitations much troubled me, and my countenance changed in me: but I kept the matter in my heart.

In verses 1-7 Daniel is essentially repeating his description of world empires that he first described in Dan 2. He interpreted the dream of King Nebuchadnezzar in chapter 2 and in chapter 7 it is Daniel who has the dream. One big difference in the two dreams was that the King's dream consisted of a metallic image while Daniel's dream consisted of animals.

In verse 8 Daniel describes the rise of the antichrist. The account of the rise of antichrist does not continue in verse 9. Instead, verse 9 and 10 describe events which are very similar to those described by John which immediately follow the Rapture in Rev 4. So, in his dream, Daniel is seeing the rise of antichrist and the Rapture at the same time or almost the same time. A comparable situation would be where you were watching a television program and suddenly switched the channel for a few moments and then switched back to the original program. You would be witnessing two things happening simultaneously. This is what happened in Daniel's vision. Then, in verse 11 Daniel continues with his narrative regarding the rise of antichrist. Daniel does not understand the vision so in verse 16 an angel comes to his aid to interpret the dream. The angel tells Daniel in verse 18 what will be the end of the matter- "the saints of the Most High shall take the kingdom, and possess the kingdom for ever, even for ever and ever."

To further understand the vision we need to identify who the saints are and which kingdom is being referred to in verse 18. The kingdom is the easiest to identify and from verse 18 we know that the kingdom is eternal because it lasts forever. Verse 14 tells us that the kingdom is over all people, nations, and languages and can never be destroyed. Verse 27 confirms what is said in verses 14 and 18.

The next question to address is who the saints in the vision are. It is said in verse 18 and 27 that the kingdom and dominion shall be given to the saints of the Most High, whose kingdom is an everlasting kingdom, and all dominions shall serve and obey him. The Jews and gentiles who are born again believers are the saints referred to in Daniel's vision. They are the ones who accompany Christ when he returns to possess the kingdom. They will rule with

Christ over the entire kingdom. This event is described in Rev 19:11-14.

Revelation 19:11-14

¹¹ And I saw heaven opened, and behold a white horse; and he that sat upon him was called Faithful and True, and in righteousness he doth judge and make war.

¹² His eyes were as a flame of fire, and on his head were many crowns; and he had a name written, that no man knew, but he himself.

¹³ And he was clothed with a vesture dipped in blood: and his name is called The Word of God.

¹⁴ And the armies which were in heaven followed him upon white horses, clothed in fine linen, white and clean.

Some commentators say that the saints in these verses in Daniel 7 refer to the Jews and it then follows that the kingdom is Israel. I hope the analysis in the paragraphs above shows otherwise. The Jews who are alive when Jesus returns at the end of the seven-year tribulation for Israel (Daniel's 70th week) will be saved when they gaze upon Him who they have pierced and will be restored to the land given to them through the Abrahamic Covenant (Zechariah 12:10). They are part of the everlasting kingdom given to the saints of the Most High. Daniels 70th week is beyond the scope of this book so it won't be discussed further in the main part of the book. However, because of it's close proximity to the Rapture and the return of Jesus, I have included a discussion of Daniel's 70th week as Appendix A in the back of the book.

Now back to Antichrist. His exploits are explained by the angel and in verse 21 and 25 the angel states that the antichrist made war with the saints and prevailed against them for a period of 42 months. (In verse 25 the phrase "time and times and a dividing of time" means 1 year plus 2 years plus ½ year equals 3 ½ years or 42 months.) This is essentially the same thing that happens to the saints in the Olivet Discourse and in Revelation starting with the removal of the fifth seal. We are now told that the persecution lasts 42 months. This can be confirmed in Revelation 12:14 where the tribulation or left behind saints are pursued by the antichrist for 42months.

Revelation 12:1-17

And there appeared a great wonder in heaven; <u>a woman clothed with the sun,</u> and the moon under her feet, and upon her head a crown of twelve stars:
² And <u>she being with child cried, travailing in birth, and pained to be delivered.</u>
³ And there appeared <u>another wonder in heaven</u>; and behold a great <u>red dragon, having seven heads and ten horns, and seven crowns upon his heads.</u>
⁴ And his tail drew the third part of the stars of heaven, and did cast them to the earth: and <u>the dragon stood before the woman which was ready to be delivered, for to devour her child as soon as it was born</u>.
⁵ And <u>she brought forth a man child, who was to rule all nations with a rod of iron: and her child was caught up unto God</u>, and to his throne.

⁶ And <u>the woman fled into the wilderness, where she hath a place prepared of God, that they should feed her there a thousand two hundred and threescore days.</u>

⁷ And <u>there was war in heaven: Michael and his angels fought against the dragon; and the dragon fought and his angels,</u>

⁸ And <u>prevailed not; neither was their place found any more in heaven.</u>

⁹ <u>And the great dragon was cast out, that old serpent, called the Devil, and Satan, which deceiveth the whole world: he was cast out into the earth, and his angels were cast out with him.</u>

¹⁰ And I heard a loud voice saying in heaven, Now is come salvation, and strength, and the kingdom of our God, and the power of his Christ: for <u>the accuser of our brethren is cast down, which accused them before our God day and night.</u> (the saints are caught up and Satan is cast down)

¹¹ And they overcame him by the blood of the Lamb, and by the word of their testimony; and they loved not their lives unto the death.

¹² Therefore rejoice, ye heavens, and ye that dwell in them. <u>Woe to the inhabiters of the earth and of the sea! for the devil is come down unto you, having great wrath, because he knoweth that he hath but a short time.</u>

¹³ And when the dragon saw that he was cast unto the earth, he persecuted the woman which brought forth the man child.

¹⁴ And to the woman were given two wings of a great eagle, that she might fly into the wilderness, into her place, where she is nourished for a time, and times, and half a time, from the face of the serpent.

¹⁵ And the serpent cast out of his mouth water as a flood after the woman, that he might cause her to be carried away of the flood.

¹⁶ And the earth helped the woman, and the earth opened her mouth, and swallowed up the flood which the dragon cast out of his mouth.

¹⁷ And the <u>dragon was wroth with the woman, and went to make war with the remnant of her seed</u>, which keep the commandments of God, and have the testimony of Jesus Christ. (remnant is left behind saints)

Chapters 4-10 in Revelation describe consecutive events. They start in chapter 4 with the Rapture of the Church and end in chapter 10 with the return of Jesus to reclaim the earth and evict Satan. Chapter 12 supplies more details of the Rapture and it tells the activities of Satan when he is cast down to the earth at the time of the Rapture.

Verse 1 of chapter 12 is hard to understand. Reading the chapter as a whole one can conclude that the woman in verse 1 is the Church and she is shining brightly. In verse 2 she is about to deliver a child and the immediate impulse is to assume that the child is Jesus. If that is the case then the woman in verse 1 would be Mary. However, the following verses confirm that the woman is the Church and she is giving birth to the raptured saints. In verse 3 the great dragon is unmistakably Satan. In verses 4-10 the action starts. Michael, the arch angel, rises up to fight Satan. Michael prevails and Satan plus one third of the angels are cast down to the earth. Satan is trying to prevent the Rapture but he fails. The raptured church, referred to as the man child, was caught up to God on His throne. This is a perfect description of the Rapture. Verse 6 says that the women, minus the raptured saints, fled to the wilderness where they are cared for by God for a period of 1230 days.

Verse 13 and 14 tell us that the dragon purses the woman, individuals who become believers after the Rapture, for a time, times, and a dividing of time (42 months). This is the same amount of time that is indicated in Daniel's vision described in Daniel 7. Verse 17 shows the hatred that the dragon has for the left behind Saints and his desire to destroy them.

The answer to the third question is that the Rapture will happen after the signs that precede the beginning of the end. Immediately following the Rapture there is a worship service in heaven followed by the seal judgments and the preaching of the Gospel to all people on the earth. Those people who are saved through the preaching of the Gospel will be hated, persecuted, and killed for their testimony. Some of the saved may survive. The persecution of tribulation saints will continue for 42 months and then the end of the Church Age will come.

QUESTION 4

What time is it now?

So far, we have answered three of the four questions. We have used scripture to describe the Rapture and to tell us why it is necessary. We have also shown in the general timeline of the Olivet Discourse when the Rapture will occur. The only question remaining is **What time is it now?** Paul addressed that question in 1Thes 5:1 when he told the Thessalonians "But of the times and the seasons, brethren, ye have no need that I write unto you." Paul had given them information so that they could identify the times and seasons. They did not know the day or the hour so he told them to watch and be sober. This is still the best advice for believers to follow while waiting for the Rapture of the Church.

The Olivet Discourse in Matthew 24 will be relied upon to help answer that question.

Matthew 24:3-36 (v.3-6 are the signs that precede the beginning of the end)

³ And as he sat upon the mount of Olives, the disciples came unto him privately, saying, Tell us, when shall these things be? and what shall be the sign of thy coming, and of the end of the world?

⁴ And Jesus answered and said unto them, Take heed that no man deceive you.

⁵ For many shall come in my name, saying, I am Christ; and shall deceive many.

⁶ And ye shall hear of wars and rumours of wars: see that ye be not troubled: for all these things must come to pass, but the end is not yet. (v. 7-14 are immediately after the rapture of the church and last until the end of the church age. Total time for v.7-14 is 42 months)

⁷ For nation shall rise against nation, and kingdom against kingdom: and there shall be famines, and pestilences, and earthquakes, in divers places.

⁸ All these are the beginning of sorrows.

⁹ Then shall they deliver you up to be afflicted, and shall kill you: and ye shall be hated of all nations for my name's sake.

¹⁰ And then shall many be offended, and shall betray one another, and shall hate one another.

¹¹ And many false prophets shall rise, and shall deceive many.

¹² And because iniquity shall abound, the love of many shall wax cold.

¹³ But he that shall endure unto the end, the same shall be saved.

¹⁴ And this gospel of the kingdom shall be preached in all the world for a witness unto all nations; and then shall the end come.

¹⁵ When ye therefore shall see the abomination of desolation, spoken of by Daniel the prophet, stand in the holy place, (whoso readeth, let him understand:)

¹⁶ Then let them which be in Judaea flee into the mountains:

¹⁷ Let him which is on the housetop not come down to take any thing out of his house:

¹⁸ Neither let him which is in the field return back to take his clothes.

¹⁹ And woe unto them that are with child, and to them that give suck in those days!

²⁰ But pray ye that your flight be not in the winter, neither on the sabbath day:

²¹ For then shall be great tribulation, such as was not since the beginning of the world to this time, no, nor ever shall be.

²² And except those days should be shortened, there should no flesh be saved: but for the elect's sake those days shall be shortened.

²³ Then if any man shall say unto you, Lo, here is Christ, or there; believe it not.

²⁴ For there shall arise false Christs, and false prophets, and shall shew great signs and wonders; insomuch that, if it were possible, they shall deceive the very elect.

²⁵ Behold, I have told you before.

²⁶ Wherefore if they shall say unto you, Behold, he is in the desert; go not forth: behold, he is in the secret chambers; believe it not.

²⁷ For as the lightning cometh out of the east, and shineth even unto the west; so shall also the coming of the Son of man be.

^{28} *For wheresoever the carcase is, there will the eagles be gathered together.*

^{29} *Immediately after the tribulation of those days shall the sun be darkened, and the moon shall not give her light, and the stars shall fall from heaven, and the powers of the heavens shall be shaken:*

^{30} *And then shall appear the sign of the Son of man in heaven: and then shall all the tribes of the earth mourn, and they shall see the Son of man coming in the clouds of heaven with power and great glory.*

^{31} *And he shall send his angels with a great sound of a trumpet, and they shall gather together his elect from the four winds, from one end of heaven to the other.*

^{32} *Now learn a parable of the fig tree; When his branch is yet tender, and putteth forth leaves, ye know that summer is nigh:*

^{33} *So likewise ye, when ye shall see all these things, know that it is near, even at the doors.*

^{34} *Verily I say unto you, This generation shall not pass, till all these things be fulfilled.*

^{35} *Heaven and earth shall pass away, but my words shall not pass away.*

^{36} *But of that day and hour knoweth no man, no, not the angels of heaven, but my Father only.*

In Matthew 24 Jesus was answering the question "what shall be the sign of thy coming, and of the end of the world?" He answers those questions in verses 4-6 and they become the signs that precede the beginning of the end of the age and the return of Christ. The two signs are 1. "many shall come in my name, saying, I am Christ; and shall deceive many." and, 2. "ye shall hear of wars and rumors of wars;".

Douglas Hamp has written three articles that are published on the Rapture Ready web site (raptureready.com) making the case that those two signs have happened in the twentieth century. I recommend that you read his articles.

He says that since 1900 there have been many dozens who have either claimed to be Jesus or the Christ in one form or another. He says that some of the most notable are Sun Myung Moon, David Koresh, Ariffin Mohamed, and Sergei Torop. Add to this a very large number of New Age followers who all consider themselves to be God. This movement was made popular by celebrities such as Shirley MacLaine in the 1980's.

Regarding war, he states that only in the twentieth century have we seen the entire world at war, not just once but twice. The estimated military and civilian death toll for the two world wars is 75-100 million people, a number unheard of before in human history. The past century could easily be described as wars and rumors of wars. I believe that both of these signs reached their fullness in the late 1980's.

In addition to the signs there were two bellwether events that occurred during back to back weeks in October 1990. During the first week East and West Germany were unified and on Monday of the second week the Temple Mount Faithful attempted to lay the cornerstone for the new temple in Jerusalem. The day is commonly known as Black Monday. The unification of Germany was necessary for the revival of the Roman Empire. Five other nations; Poland, Rumania, Bulgaria, Hungary, and Czechoslovakia had been plucked away from the Communist bloc in the previous year to also become part of the revived Roman Empire. These events represent a juncture in the road and point forward to the fulfillment of Bible prophecy involving the revival of the Roman Empire and the building of the new Temple on the Temple Mount, both of which are necessary for the return of Christ. I believe these two events mark the end of the period of time necessary to produce the signs in Mat 24:4-6 and to mark a change in future direction.

So where have we arrived? This brings us to the last sentence of Mat 24:6 which states "for all these things must come to pass, but the end is not yet." There is an indefinite period of time between the end of verse 6 and the beginning of verse 7. That is where we are right now and have been since October 1990. Verses 7-14 are the beginning of the end of the age. They, and the rest of the chapter, are the verses for which the signs are given. The events described in 7-14 are the same as those described in Rev 6 and 7 which are after the rapture. I covered the same material in answer to one of the previous questions and will not do so again.

This now gives us a partial answer to the question, **What Time Is It Now?** The point in time that we are at right now is that the signs have occurred and the rapture follows in verse 7. If that doesn't take your breath away nothing will. It is more important now than ever before to follow Paul's instruction to "watch."

There are two other portions of the Olivet Discourse that will help answer the question, **What Time Is It Now?** In Mat 24:32-35 Jesus gives us the parable of the fig tree and in Mat 24:36-39 He says that world conditions just prior to his return will be "as the days of Noah were.... before the flood."

Matthew 24:32-35

[32] Now learn a parable of the fig tree; When his branch is yet tender, and putteth forth leaves, ye know that summer is nigh:

[33] So likewise ye, when ye shall see all these things, know that it is near, even at the doors.

[34] Verily I say unto you, This generation shall not pass, till all these things be fulfilled.

[35] Heaven and earth shall pass away, but my words shall not pass away.

The fig tree parable is important because if we understand what the fig tree symbolizes and if we know when it put forth leaves then we can know that the return of Christ will occur within a generation.

The first question that needs to be answered is what is meant by "till all these things be fulfilled." at the end of verse 34. Is Jesus including the signs that precede the beginning of the end or is He excluding them and starting from the beginning of the end? This is an important question because including the signs would make the time from beginning of the signs until the return of Christ much longer than a generation. I believe that he was saying that the generation would not pass until the events starting in verse 7 through 31 happened. This would mean that there is not a time limit for the signs to occur, separating the signs from the rest of the chapter. Verse 6 supports that position when it says, referring to the signs, "for all these things must come to pass, but the end is not yet."

The next question that needs to be answered is what is meant by the fig tree. Again, I want to refer you to the three articles written by Douglas Hamp. He summarizes evidence from scripture and concludes that the fig tree is unmistakably Israel. I urge you to read his first article. The majority of commentaries agree with him and so do I. Israel, the fig tree sign, was born on May 14, 1948. Keep that date in mind.

The last question has to do with the length of a generation and is important because the parable tells us that Christ will return in the life span of a generation beginning with the birth of Israel. The parable actually says that "This generation shall not pass, till all these things be fulfilled." Commentators have different opinions on what this means. Some say that it refers to the average life span of a person and others say that it means that at least some people of the generation will live to see the return of Jesus. I believe that the part of the verse that says "This generation shall not pass" leads one to conclude that he is saying that Christ will return near the end of the generation. It is similar to telling someone that something will happen before the end of the week or that something will happen before you pass away. The reasonable expectation in these examples is that it will happen near the end of the week or near the end of the life. It is reasonable to conclude that the generation that began at the birth of Israel is "this generation" and it will not pass until Jesus returns. At least some people of that generation will be alive to see His return.

At the present time Israel is 72 years old. Those born in 1948 are also 72. If the Rapture happened today then Christ would not return for another 10 ½ years, making those born in 1948 either 82 or 83 upon His return. I am using 10 ½ years because I believe that there is a tribulation for the left behind saints for a period of 42 months after the Rapture. Both Daniel 7 and Revelation 12 support that position. I have described this in answer to one of the previous questions. The end of the church age comes at the end of the 42 months. Romans 11:25 and 26 indicate that blindness, for the most part, is happened to Israel until the fullness of the gentiles is accomplished. That fullness happens at the end of the Church Age. *[25] For I would not, brethren, that ye should be ignorant of this mystery, lest ye should be wise in your own conceits; that blindness in part is happened to Israel, until the fulness of the Gentiles be come in. [26] And so all Israel shall be saved: as it is written, There shall come out of Sion the Deliverer, and shall turn away ungodliness from Jacob*: Daniels 70th week (a 7-year period) for Israel follows closely after the end of the church age, making the length of time between the Rapture and the return of Christ to be 10 ½ years. Daniel 12 in Appendix A identifies three periods of 3 ½ years from the Rapture to the return of Jesus with His Saints.

If the Rapture does not happen for another 8 years from now (2028), those born in 1948 will be 90 or 91 at the return of Christ. According to the U.S. Census Bureau, 3.6% of the population was age 80 or greater in 2010. Only 1.7% of the population was 85 or greater. Only .6% of the population was 90 or greater. Time is definitely running out for the generation born in 1948.

Table 1.
Population 65 Years and Older by Age and Sex: 2000 and 2010
(For information on confidentiality protection, nonsampling error, and definitions, see www.census.gov/prod/cen2010/doc/sf1.pdf)

Sex and age	2000			2010			Change, 2000 to 2010	
	Number	Percentage of 65 years and over population	Percentage of U.S. total population	Number	Percentage of 65 years and over population	Percentage of U.S. total population	Number	Percentage
Both sexes, all ages	281,421,906	(X)	100.0	308,745,538	(X)	100.0	27,323,632	9.7
65 years and over	34,991,753	100.0	12.4	40,267,984	100.0	13.0	5,276,231	15.1
65 to 74 years	18,390,986	52.6	6.5	21,713,429	53.9	7.0	3,322,443	18.1
65 to 69 years	9,533,545	27.2	3.4	12,435,263	30.9	4.0	2,901,718	30.4
70 to 74 years	8,857,441	25.3	3.1	9,278,166	23.0	3.0	420,725	4.7
75 to 84 years	12,361,180	35.3	4.4	13,061,122	32.4	4.2	699,942	5.7
75 to 79 years	7,415,813	21.2	2.6	7,317,795	18.2	2.4	−98,018	−1.3
80 to 84 years	4,945,367	14.1	1.8	5,743,327	14.3	1.9	797,960	16.1
85 to 94 years	3,902,349	11.2	1.4	5,068,825	12.6	1.6	1,166,476	29.9
85 to 89 years	2,789,818	8.0	1.0	3,620,459	9.0	1.2	830,641	29.8
90 to 94 years	1,112,531	3.2	0.4	1,448,366	3.6	0.5	335,835	30.2
95 years and over	337,238	1.0	0.1	424,608	1.1	0.1	87,370	25.9
95 to 99 years	286,784	0.8	0.1	371,244	0.9	0.1	84,460	29.5
100 years and over	50,454	0.1	—	53,364	0.1	—	2,910	5.8
Median age, 65 years and over...........	74.5	(X)	(X)	74.1	(X)	(X)	−0.4	(X)

69

Matthew 24:36-39

36 But of that day and hour knoweth no man, no, not the angels of heaven, but my Father only.

37 But as the days of Noah were, so shall also the coming of the Son of man be.

38 For as in the days that were before the flood they were eating and drinking, marrying and giving in marriage, until the day that Noe entered into the ark,

39 And knew not until the flood came, and took them all away; so shall also the coming of the Son of man be. (Luke 21:36, we are to pray that we are counted worthy to escape all these things that shall come to pass)

Luke 17:28-30

28 Likewise also as it was in the days of Lot; they did eat, they drank, they bought, they sold, they planted, they builded;

29 But the same day that Lot went out of Sodom it rained fire and brimstone from heaven, and destroyed them all.

30 Even thus shall it be in the day when the Son of man is revealed.

Many commentaries have been written about the above verses comparing conditions before the flood to conditions now. Most of the commentaries state that even though there was some normalcy involved in Noah's time, as verse 38 of Matthew 24 above indicates, the times were also exceedingly wicked and included unholy marriage. That was the reason for judgment in the form of a flood. Genesis 6 describes conditions on the earth and says that Noah and his family found grace in the eyes of the Lord and that is why God did not destroy them in the flood. All other human and animal life was destroyed by the flood. The same situation existed in Sodom and Gomorrah where sexual sin was rampant. Lot and his family were rescued from the city just prior to its destruction by fire.

Are we currently in the time called "as the days of Noah were"? I believe that we are and that we have been for some time. Many articles have been written describing how wicked and vile we have become and many have warned that this will result in God's judgment against us. I agree.

Without repeating the descriptions of how wicked our society has become we should take notice of the speed at which two examples of wickedness have become accepted in society. The homosexual lifestyle and gay marriage were fringe movements in society in the early 1990's. "Don't ask, don't tell" was still the accepted norm for the military and society as a whole until the last few years. Now you can serve as openly gay in the military and elsewhere and any person advocating the non-gay lifestyle will be severely chastised. The same situation exists for gay marriage. In 1996 the Congress and President endorsed the Defense of marriage Act (DOMA) which allowed states to deny gay marriage. Recently the Supreme Court of the United States has ruled that same sex marriage is the law of the land.

God will have the last word on this matter, not the Supreme Court.

Isaiah 5:20

²⁰ Woe unto them that call evil good, and good evil; that put darkness for light, and light for darkness; that put bitter for sweet, and sweet for bitter!

The Bible identifies homosexuality and sexual perversion as sin and as an abomination. Noah and his family were saved when the Lord destroyed the world with a flood and Lot and his family were saved when the Lord destroyed Sodom and Gomorrah with fire. Likewise, the Lord will rescue true believers with the Rapture before he delivers His wrath upon the world in these end of the days. Sin and wickedness will again be the trigger for the rapture.

Wickedness in society, including homosexuality and gay marriage, is increasing at an accelerated rate and is being accepted as normal even as we continue in everyday activities that we have always done. This is definitely a sign that we are in a time called "as the days of Noah were."

CONCLUSION

So, **What Time Is It Now?** The answer is that we do not know the exact time but we do know that time is running out. The generation of the fig tree, Israel, is running to an end and we are in the time identified in the Bible "as the days of Noah were." You can make your own estimate of time remaining like I have done above but the window is getting smaller each day. We are near the end of the age of Grace by any estimate. Maybe the real answer to the question, **What Time Is It Now?** is that it is time, if you have not already done so, to put your faith in Jesus so that you are not left behind at the Rapture.

Timothy E. Miller April 7, 2014

PERSONAL REFLECTIONS

I can't help but think about all the people who were following Bon's and Julie's blogs believing that the world as they knew it would soon end. Reading the statements and questions from the followers of the bloggers showed how seriously these people took the supposed messages from God that Bon and Julie were relaying to them. I could feel a sense of urgency on the part of the followers and a need to know exactly what to do. These people, at least some of them, were very vulnerable and were subject to almost any kind of deception. Reading the comments revealed that some of them were familiar with the Bible because they either quoted scripture or referred to it. I have to assume that some of them were true believers and that they were also deceived by Bon and Julie. Both of these people, Bon and Julie, also profess to be true believers and yet neither one of them bothered to research the Bible to determine if their messages from God were consistent with His Word. There is also no evidence that any of their followers questioned any of the messages from God. That is a sad state of affairs because it shows how easily people can be deceived. Whether it is a supposed message from God, a comet or strange moon in the sky, or a human prediction of the end of the world; if it can't be substantiated or confirmed by the Bible it may be wrong. As you hear more of these messages and predictions, and be assured that you will, go to the Bible to confirm or deny them. Study the Bible with a friend and become a Berean.

APPENDIX A

Daniel's 70 Weeks of Years

Daniel 9

In the first year of Darius the son of Ahasuerus, of the seed of the Medes, which was made king over the realm of the Chaldeans;

²In the first year of his reign I Daniel understood by books the number of the years, whereof the word of the LORD came to Jeremiah the prophet, that he would accomplish seventy years in the desolations of Jerusalem. (Jer 25:9-12)

³ And I set my face unto the Lord God, to seek by prayer and supplications, with fasting, and sackcloth, and ashes:

⁴ And I prayed unto the LORD my God, and made my confession, and said, O Lord, the great and dreadful God, keeping the covenant and mercy to them that love him, and to them that keep his commandments;

⁵ We have sinned, and have committed iniquity, and have done wickedly, and have rebelled, even by departing from thy precepts and from thy judgments:

6 Neither have we hearkened unto thy servants the prophets, which spake in thy name to our kings, our princes, and our fathers, and to all the people of the land.

7 O LORD, righteousness belongeth unto thee, but unto us confusion of faces, as at this day; to the men of Judah, and to the inhabitants of Jerusalem, and unto all Israel, that are near, and that are far off, through all the countries whither thou hast driven them, because of their trespass that they have trespassed against thee.

8 O Lord, to us belongeth confusion of face, to our kings, to our princes, and to our fathers, because we have sinned against thee.

9 To the Lord our God belong mercies and forgivenesses, though we have rebelled against him;

10 Neither have we obeyed the voice of the LORD our God, to walk in his laws, which he set before us by his servants the prophets.

11 Yea, all Israel have transgressed thy law, even by departing, that they might not obey thy voice; therefore the curse is poured upon us, and the oath that is written in the law of Moses the servant of God, because we have sinned against him.

12 And he hath confirmed his words, which he spake against us, and against our judges that judged us, by bringing upon us a great evil: for under the whole heaven hath not been done as hath been done upon Jerusalem.

13 As it is written in the law of Moses, all this evil is come upon us: yet made we not our prayer before the LORD our God, that we might turn from our iniquities, and understand thy truth.

¹⁴ Therefore hath the LORD watched upon the evil, and brought it upon us: for the LORD our God is righteous in all his works which he doeth: for we obeyed not his voice.

¹⁵ And now, O Lord our God, that hast brought thy people forth out of the land of Egypt with a mighty hand, and hast gotten thee renown, as at this day; we have sinned, we have done wickedly.

¹⁶ O LORD, according to all thy righteousness, I beseech thee, let thine anger and thy fury be turned away from thy city Jerusalem, thy holy mountain: because for our sins, and for the iniquities of our fathers, Jerusalem and thy people are become a reproach to all that are about us.

¹⁷ Now therefore, O our God, hear the prayer of thy servant, and his supplications, and cause thy face to shine upon thy sanctuary that is desolate, for the Lord's sake.

¹⁸ O my God, incline thine ear, and hear; open thine eyes, and behold our desolations, and the city which is called by thy name: for we do not present our supplications before thee for our righteousnesses, but for thy great mercies.

¹⁹ O Lord, hear; O Lord, forgive; O Lord, hearken and do; defer not, for thine own sake, O my God: for thy city and thy people are called by thy name.

²⁰ And whiles I was speaking, and praying, and confessing my sin and the sin of my people Israel, and presenting my supplication before the LORD my God for the holy mountain of my God;

²¹ Yea, whiles I was speaking in prayer, even the man Gabriel, whom I had seen in the vision at the beginning, being caused to fly swiftly, touched me about the time of the evening oblation.

²² And he informed me, and talked with me, and said, O Daniel, I am now come forth to give thee skill and understanding.

²³ At the beginning of thy supplications the commandment came forth, and I am come to shew thee; for thou art greatly beloved: therefore understand the matter, and consider the vision.

²⁴ Seventy weeks are determined upon thy people and upon thy holy city, to finish the transgression, and to make an end of sins, and to make reconciliation for iniquity, and to bring in everlasting righteousness, and to seal up the vision and prophecy, and to anoint the most Holy.

²⁵ Know therefore and understand, that from the going forth of the commandment to restore and to build Jerusalem unto the Messiah the Prince shall be seven weeks, and threescore and two weeks: the street shall be built again, and the wall, even in troublous times.

²⁶ And after threescore and two weeks shall Messiah be cut off, but not for himself: and the people of the prince that shall come shall destroy the city and the sanctuary; and the end thereof shall be with a flood, and unto the end of the war desolations are determined.

²⁷ And he shall confirm the covenant with many for one week: and in the midst of the week he shall cause the sacrifice and the oblation to cease, and for the overspreading of abominations he shall make it desolate, even until the consummation, and that determined shall be poured upon the desolate.

King James Version (KJV)

Question: «What are the seventy weeks of Daniel?»

Answer: The "seventy weeks" prophecy is one of the most significant and detailed Messianic prophecies of the Old Testament. It is found in <u>Daniel 9</u>. The chapter begins with Daniel praying for Israel, acknowledging the nation's sins against God and asking for God's mercy. As Daniel prayed, the angel Gabriel appeared to him and gave him a vision of Israel's future.

The Divisions of the 70 Weeks

In verse 24, Gabriel says, "Seventy 'sevens' are decreed for your people and your holy city." Almost all commentators agree that the seventy "sevens" should be understood as seventy "weeks" of years, in other words, a period of 490 years. These verses provide a sort of "clock" that gives an idea of when the Messiah would come and some of the events that would accompany His appearance.

The prophecy goes on to divide the 490 years into three smaller units: one of 49 years, one of 434 years, and one 7 years. The final "week" of 7 years is further divided in half. Verse 25 says, "From the time the word goes out to restore and rebuild Jerusalem until the Anointed One, the ruler, comes, there will be seven 'sevens,' and sixty-two 'sevens.'" Seven "sevens" is 49 years, and sixty-two "sevens" is another 434 years:

49 years + 434 years = 483 years

The Purpose of the 70 Weeks

The prophecy contains a statement concerning God's six-fold purpose in bringing these events to pass. Verse 24 says this purpose is 1) "to finish transgression," 2) "to put an end to sin," 3) "to atone for wickedness," 4) "to bring in everlasting righteousness," 5) "to seal up vision and prophecy," and 6) "to anoint the most holy."

Notice that these results concern the total eradication of sin and the establishing of righteousness. The prophecy of the 70 weeks summarizes what happens before Jesus sets up His millennial kingdom. Of special note is the third in the list of results: "to atone for wickedness." Jesus accomplished the atonement for sin by His death on the cross (Romans 3:25; Hebrews 2:17).

The Fulfillment of the 70 Weeks

Gabriel said the prophetic clock would start at the time that a decree was issued to rebuild Jerusalem. From the date of that decree to the time of the Messiah would be 483 years. We know from history that the command to "restore and rebuild Jerusalem" was given by King Artaxerxes of Persia c. 445 B.C. (see Nehemiah 2:1-8).

The first unit of 49 years (seven "sevens") covers the time that it took to rebuild Jerusalem, "with streets and a trench, but in times of trouble" (Daniel 9:25). This rebuilding is chronicled in the book of Nehemiah.

Using the Jewish custom of a 360-day year, 483 years after 445 B.C. places us at A.D. 30, which would coincide with Jesus' triumphal entry into Jerusalem (Matthew 21:1-9). The prophecy in Daniel 9 specifies that after the completion of the 483 years, "the Anointed One will be cut off" (verse 26). This was fulfilled when Jesus was crucified.

Daniel 9:26 continues with a prediction that, after the Messiah is killed, "the people of the ruler who will come will destroy the city and the sanctuary." This was fulfilled with the destruction of Jerusalem in A.D. 70. The "ruler who will come" is a reference to the Antichrist, who, it seems, will have some connection with Rome, since it was the Romans who destroyed Jerusalem.

The Final Week of the 70 Weeks

Of the 70 "sevens," 69 have been fulfilled in history. This leaves one more "seven" yet to be fulfilled. Most scholars believe that we are now living in a huge gap between the 69th week and the 70th week. The prophetic clock has been paused, as it were. The final "seven" of Daniel is what we usually call the tribulation period.

Daniel's prophecy reveals some of the actions of the Antichrist, the "ruler who will come." Verse 27 says, "He will confirm a covenant with many for one 'seven.'" However, "in the middle of the 'seven,' . . . he will set up an abomination that causes desolation" in the temple. Jesus warned of this event in Matthew 24:15. After the Antichrist breaks the covenant with Israel, a time of "great tribulation" begins (Matthew 24:21, NKJV).

Daniel also predicts that the Antichrist will face judgment. He only rules "until the end that is decreed is poured out on him" (Daniel 9:27). God will only allow evil to go so far, and the judgment the Antichrist will face has already been planned out.

Conclusion

The prophecy of the 70 weeks is complex and amazingly detailed, and much has been written about it. Of course, there are various interpretations, but what we have presented here is the <u>dispensational, premillennial</u> view. One thing is certain: God has a time table, and He is keeping things on schedule. He knows the end from the beginning (<u>Isaiah 46:10</u>), and we should always be looking for the triumphant return of our Lord (<u>Revelation 22:7</u>).

Recommended Resource: <u>Daniel: The John Walvoord Prophecy Commentary by Walvoord & Dyer</u>

So, from the review of Daniel 9 and the commentary following, we know that 69 weeks have been accomplished and we are waiting for the commencement of the 70th week. At the end of the 70th week Jesus will return to set up His millennial Kingdom. We also know that the gap between the 69th and 70th week was started with the birth of the Church at Pentecost and it is my contention that the 70th week will not begin until the end of the Church Age which will happen 3 and ½ years after the Rapture of the Church. After the Church age is ended the Lord will deal with Israel for a seven year period known as Daniels 70th week. The total time from the Rapture to the return of Jesus would then be about 10 and ½ years. The 12th chapter of Daniel Supports that position.

Daniel (KJV) the Time of the End

12 *And at that time shall Michael stand up, the great prince which standeth for the children of thy people: and there* *shall be a time of trouble, such as never was since there was a nation even to that same time: and at that time thy people shall be delivered, every one that shall be found written in the book.* (Rapture saves us from a time of trouble that never was)

² *And many of them that sleep in the dust of the earth shall awake, some to everlasting life, and some to shame and everlasting contempt.* (Resurrection)

³ *And they that be wise shall shine as the brightness of the firmament; and they that turn many to righteousness as the stars for ever and ever.* (there will be many who understand the times and will spread the word)

⁴ *But thou, O Daniel, shut up the words, and seal the book, even to the time of the end: many shall run to and fro, and knowledge shall be increased.* (Daniel did not understand. The meaning was sealed until the time of the end.)

⁵ *Then I Daniel looked, and, behold, there stood other two, the one on this side of the bank of the river, and the other on that side of the bank of the river.*

⁶ *And one said to the man clothed in linen, which was upon the waters of the river, How long shall it be to the end of these wonders?* (the question refers to the length of time for the persecution of the left behind)

⁷ *And I heard the man clothed in linen, which was upon the waters of the river, when he held up his right hand and his left hand unto heaven, and sware by him that liveth for ever that it shall be for a time, times, and an half; and when he shall have accomplished to scatter the power of the holy people, all these things shall be finished.* (persecution of those left behind is 42 months, 3 ½ years)

⁸ *And I heard, but I understood not: then said I, O my Lord, what shall be the end of these things?*

⁹ And he said, Go thy way, Daniel: for the words are closed up and sealed till the time of the end. (meaning of the words is sealed until the end of the days)

¹⁰ Many shall be purified, and made white, and tried; but the wicked shall do wickedly: and none of the wicked shall understand; but the wise shall understand. (those who are saved after the Rapture, tribulation Saints in Revelation 7:9-16)

¹¹ And from the time that the daily sacrifice shall be taken away, and the abomination that maketh desolate set up, there shall be a <u>thousand two hundred and ninety days</u>. (a period of 3 ½ years, last half of Daniels 70ᵗʰ week)

¹² Blessed is he that waiteth, and cometh to the <u>thousand three hundred and five and thirty days</u>. (first half of Daniel's 70ᵗʰ week, a little more than 3 ½ years that probably starts when antichrist signs a 7 year treaty with Israel)

¹³ But go thou thy way till the end be: for thou shalt rest, and stand in thy lot at the end of the days.

Daniel identifies 3 periods of time after the rapture, each approximately 3 ½ years.

MY SALVATION IS JESUS CHRIST

The great cause of being separated from God is my own sin. The actual deliverance from this condition and salvation is Jesus Christ. Matt 18:11 "For the Son of man has come to save that which was lost." Christ redeems and saves us out of our condition by His power through the Holy Spirit.

1. Conviction of sin is the first act of Christ's power. John 16: 8 & 9

The Holy Spirit convinces us that we have no faith and are under the dominion of sin. The sense of sin and misery is revealed to us by the Spirit wounding or pricking our heart as He did in Acts 2:37. He did the same to David, Paul, and Isaiah. The conviction of sin comes in the form of particular sins and our sinful condition and the great evil of those sins. We also become aware of the punishment that follows those sins; death. Our sinful condition that we have now become aware of was imputed to us through the first Adam when Satan overthrew him in the Garden. The true spirit of conviction binds the understanding that it cannot struggle against God anymore. However, there are some who, even though they become aware of their sins, never become convinced of their sentence for them. This is just rational conviction and not spiritual. Real conviction results in the least sin, like a speck in the eye, to be very troubling. Everyone does not have the same measure of conviction, yet all the elect must have enough to attain the end of conviction, compunction.

2. Compunction, or the sense of sin, is the second act of Christ's power. Luke 7: 36-38, 2 Corinthians 7: 8-10

Conviction is the understanding of sin and compunction is the sense of it and is seated in the affections and will. As already stated, a person may have knowledge of sin without sorrow for it but for all the elect compunction immediately follows conviction (Acts2:37). The Spirit does not work the same amount of compunction in all that He saves, but only the amount that is fit for that soul. Each heart has different needs and only the Spirit knows what they are. The pricking of the heart, the wounding of the soul, causes so much fear, sorrow, guilt, and misery for sin that it causes the soul to separate from sin. It drives us away from sin and changes the unwilling to willing. It makes the soul humble and capable of union with Christ. This compunction cuts away the old Adam and makes way for the grafting of the new Adam. So, being cut from sin, we are left in a humble condition, ready for union with Christ.

3. Humiliation is the third act of Christ's power.

Conviction and compunction wounds the heart and cuts it off from evil (sin). Then humiliation will cut it off from conceit and self-confidence. We realize that we cannot save ourselves from this predicament and cry out "what must I do to be saved." If not for this omnipotent work of the Spirit we, with our proud heart, would surely provide our own cure. We would not bow down on our own. The Spirit shows us the corruption in our soul and tells us that all that we do is defiled with sin. When we fear that we have lost Christ and experience the sinking feeling that all is lost, the soul is humbled, ready to submit to the redeeming work of Christ. Humiliation says, use me as you wish. Like conviction and compunction, humiliation comes in an amount necessary for the elect to respond to the call of Christ to come unto Him for rest. If the Lord does not sever your sin in compunction and empty you from yourself in humiliation, you cannot receive Christ.

4.   The fourth act of Christ's power is the work of faith.

Faith begins with God's call and ends with our answer. The soul of the elect is unable to respond to the call before conviction, compunction, and humiliation. The nature of the call is in the form of the Word, spoken or written, ministry of men, or visions and inspirations of God. Faith is brought about by a creating power and is irresistible. The Spirit puts a necessity upon the call that overpowers us. That is why the Scripture credits Jesus with being the Author and Finisher of our faith. The soul or heart is the subject of the inward call. Many hear the outward call and never respond. But no man can come to the Lord (respond to the call) except the Father draws him, John 6:44. By faith we are grafted in or united with Christ and the result or end of faith is life eternal. Born again! Sorrow is then turned to Joy!

I will spare the details but this is how I came to Christ during the summer of 1988. I did not come on my own but only through the strong hand of Christ. I did not fully understand what had transpired but through the works of Thomas Shepard, Jonathan Edwards, John Bunyan, and others I was able to understand the salvation of Jesus Christ.

Printed in the United States
by Baker & Taylor Publisher Services